Diary of a Functioning Burnout

How to Honor Your CAPACITY and Balance Your Life

Melanie Sodka

CAPACITY CREATOR
publishing

Capacity Creator Publishing

Capacity Creator Publishing
Wainfleet, Ontario, Canada

Published 2024
ISBN-13: 978-1-0689454-1-0 (softcover)   ISBN-13: 978-1-0689454-0-3 (hardcover) ISBN-13: 978-1-0689454-2-7 (ebook) ISBN-13: 978-1-0689454-3-4 (audiobook)

This book is the author's opinion and is intended for informational purposes only. It should not be considered as a substitute for consultation with a licensed professional.

Confidential and Proprietary Material
This manuscript, titled Diary of a Functioning Burnout, is the unpublished work of Melanie Sodka. It contains confidential and proprietary information. By accepting this manuscript, you agree not to distribute, copy, or share it without the express permission of the author. All rights to this manuscript, including the rights to any accompanying materials, are reserved. Please handlethis document responsibly and with discretion.

To my husband Chris. My children Camilla and Maddox. To my parents and baby brother Gregory, an angel who is always with us. And to my family and friends. xo

Contents

Preface

I n a world where the relentless pursuit of more is the norm, many of us find ourselves stretched thin, overwhelmed, and disconnected from our true purpose. What once brought joy and meaning has become an endless list of obligations, leaving us with little capacity to focus on what truly matters. We've mastered the art of saying "yes" to everything, but in doing so, we've lost the ability to prioritize what's important.

This book isn't about time management or task organization—it's about reclaiming your life from the chaos, redefining productivity, and learning to honor your personal capacity. Drawing from both personal experience and professional insight, we'll explore the unseen forces that push us toward burnout. Together, we'll unravel the layers of overwhelm, offering a roadmap to regain control and balance.

Through these pages, you'll discover the power of saying "no" with confidence and the liberation that comes from aligning your commitments with your core values. You'll learn how to sift through the endless sea of options and distractions to cultivate a life that is not only busy but truly fulfilling.

This isn't a call to slow down—it's an invitation to engage with your life more intentionally. Your capacity is your greatest asset, and this book will guide you in mastering it. Prepare to transform the way you work, live, and connect with the world. It's time to step into your power, embrace your limits, and find balance in your pursuit of success.

For years, I felt the pressure to write 'THE book.' It wasn't until my husband gently reminded me of the weight that comes with such a pursuit that I realized the importance of letting go of that expectation. This book is not about perfection—it's about sharing real stories, including my own, and insights from others who have generously shared their experiences.

Within these chapters, you'll encounter themes of grief, laughter, burnout, love, ambition, and more—threads that weave together the tapestry of the human experience. I invite you to explore whichever chapter resonates with you, knowing that not everyone will read this book cover to cover.

I am honored that you've chosen to join me on this journey.

PART 1: AUDIT YOUR CAPACITY

Chapter One

Am I a Functioning Burnout?

Burnout isn't due to a lack of motivation. It's caused by a shortage of capacity. There are more interesting people and projects than hours in the day. The key question isn't whether you have interest. It's whether you have bandwidth. Enthusiasm is boundless. Time is finite.
— Adam Grant

Diary Entry

*T*oday, we worked long hours again, pushing ourselves beyond reasonable limits. I'm so exhausted and miserable, but I can't even pinpoint why. My days have become a blur of endless tasks and obligations, leaving me with a deep sense of fatigue that no amount of sleep seems to cure.

I find myself wishing for an escape, even fantasizing about getting into a car accident just so I could rest in a hospital bed. The thought of that feels shocking and selfish, and I feel immense guilt for even considering it. But I can't deny it—I'm just so overwhelmed and exhausted. I'm desperate for any reprieve from this relentless grind. I don't know what to do.

A Negotiation with My Doctor

I was practically a VIP at my doctor's office, visiting more times than I want to admit. I was losing hair faster than my dog shed in summer, migraines were a regular occurrence, and spontaneous bloody noses were becoming my party trick. Throw in some random bouts of cellulitis, skin rashes, and fatigue, and you've got a volatile health mocktail going on.

Desperate for a quick fix, I was hoping for a prescription that would magically solve everything. Spoiler alert: there are no magic pills. The doctor looked at me and said, "Melanie, you need rest. I'm prescribing you a month away from work."

"A month?" I blurted out, like she had just told me I had to eat brussels sprouts for every meal. I looked at her, blinked, and handed the prescription back. "How about a week?" I tried, thinking I was being clever. She stared at me, eyebrows raised, probably wondering if I had lost my mind along with my hair. That look of hers made me feel like a kid caught with their hand in the cookie jar. Reluctantly, I took the note and left.

Deep down, I knew what had been happening all along. I just didn't want to admit it. Burnout. The big, ugly B-word.

On my way home from that appointment, my phone rang. It was a call from an awards committee. The person on the other end was bubbling with excitement, eager to inform me that I had won the prestigious 40 Under 40 Award. It was a moment that should have filled me with pride and joy. I pulled over on the highway, right across from a golf course, to take the call. But instead of feeling elated, I felt numb.

The irony was stark. Here I was, being recognized for my achievements and hard work, while simultaneously grappling with the devastating effects of that very work. I was on the brink of collapse, my body manifesting the stress through physical symptoms. Sadly, I had even experienced a miscarriage without knowing I was pregnant. And now, with a burnout diagnosis and a prescription for a month-long break, I could only feel a hollow emptiness where pride and excitement should have been.

This moment was a powerful reality check. Despite all the symptoms and the clear message from my doctor, I still struggled to accept that my workaholism was the root cause of my ailments. I didn't want to believe that working too much and too hard could lead to such severe consequences. But as I sat there, parked on the side of the highway, I had to confront the reality that my relentless drive was unsustainable.

This experience taught me that success and recognition are hollow if they come at the expense of my health and well-being. It was a painful but necessary lesson that forced me to reevaluate my priorities and understand that true achievement includes taking care of oneself.

Society doesn't celebrate self-care. There are no awards, no vacations, no monetary incentives, no public recognition for taking care of ourselves. But when we work harder, achieve more, do more with less, overachieve, work weekends, sacrifice time with loved ones, lead teams, participate in multiple committees, and put in extra hours, we are sometimes rewarded. These rewards—recognition, accolades, promotions, extra money, incentives—are dangled before us, driving us to push even harder.

This is what we've been taught to strive for: the glorification of the grind, the relentless pursuit of success. We've collectively created and upheld this hustle culture, where our worth is measured by our productivity and sacrifices. It took me three intense bouts of burnout to finally break free from this cycle.

What Is a Functioning Burnout?

One clear indicator that I was a functioning burnout was my relentless habit of squeezing activities into any available slot in my calendar. Whenever I found a gap, I felt compelled to fill it with commitments. We are fortunate to have many family members and friends we enjoy spending time with, but this blessing also became a source of pressure for me. I had a challenging time saying no whenever someone invited me to do something. My husband often attributes this to my FOMO (fear of missing out), but a significant part of it was my tendency to be a people pleaser.

Being a people pleaser and struggling with the inability to say no are major factors that erode our capacities. You may constantly feel that if you decline an invitation, you are letting someone down, and you consider this unacceptable. The result is overcommitting and trying to squeeze people into your schedule, giving them only a fraction of your attention.

Looking back, I am embarrassed by this behavior. I realize now that attempting to do too many things at once meant I was not truly present for anyone. I was giving people less than they deserved, which is unfair because offering your full attention is one of the greatest gifts you can give. This realization has come with age and experience, teaching me the importance of setting boundaries and valuing quality over quantity in my interactions.

Pressing Your Luck

The patterns and habits of a functioning burnout are not easily remedied. In fact, they continued as I transitioned out of corporate to become a full-time college professor. I was teaching entrepreneurship while trying to be an entrepreneur myself. I recall a particular incident when I had scheduled a crucial meeting with my dean. However, I had also committed to flying out to see a client on the same day. Determined to do it all, I booked my flight with just enough time to drive back to the office and make it to the meeting right after landing.

This plan was cutting it close, and I didn't inform anyone at the college about my tight schedule. I wasn't doing anything wrong per se, but I knew it might not be viewed favorably if my dean found out I was squeezing in a client visit before our meeting. Nonetheless, I was so focused on fitting everything in that I didn't consider the lack of contingency. If my flight had been delayed, I would have had no explanation for my dean. But at that moment, all I could think was, *I'll make it work.*

Remarkably, I did manage to show up at the meeting with one minute to spare, albeit slightly winded. This incident epitomizes the functioning burnout mindset—trying to do everything, scheduling back-to-back commitments, and relying on the belief that sheer willpower will make everything fall into place. The reality is far less glamorous: it's stressful and risky.

Addiction to Being Busy

This addiction to being busy, this need to get everything done, are a hallmark of a functioning burnout. They create a false sense of accomplishment and mask the actual cost—strained relationships, missed opportunities for meaningful interaction, and a perpetually stressed state of mind. Only later do the ramifications become clear, often leading to regret and a profound sense of having missed out on profoundly important moments.

A person who is a functioning burnout—defined as an individual experiencing severe mental and physical strain from chronic work stress yet continuing to perform job responsibilities—maintains a facade of normalcy despite their significant underlying issues. There is a notable decline in cognitive abilities, physiological health, and overall quality of life, masked by the outward continuation of daily responsibilities. Table 1.1 highlights the importance of understanding the root causes of stress and addiction in order to prevent severe long-term consequences.

Aspect	Consequence
Cognitive Function	Significant impact on cognitive abilities, including executive functions such as decision-making, problem-solving and memory.
Physiological Health	Adverse effects such as increased heart rate, hypertension, decreased physical activity, sleep disturbances, weakened immune function and higher risk of cardiovascular diseases.
Quality of Life	Diminished overall quality of life with symptoms of depression, anxiety and dissatisfaction affecting personal relationships and social life.
Daily Functioning	Work duties fulfilled often by masking significant underlying strain at the expense of well-being.

Table 1.1. Aspects and Consequences of the Behaviors of a Functioning Burnout

Functioning burnout behaviors showed up in my life as a mom in ways that, looking back, are heartbreaking. I remember flipping through old photos from a time during my second bout of burnout. I was juggling roles as a college professor and entrepreneur, as well as commuting regularly and being a mom to two young kids. As I looked through those pictures, I noticed a pattern—many of the photos with my kids showed us lying down together. On the surface, these moments looked like sweet, snuggly times, but deep down, I knew the truth.

I often chose to lie down with my kids because I was utterly exhausted. It was the only way I could manage to spend time with them. I gave everything to my work and came home with nothing left in reserve. I would be depleted, barely able to muster the energy to play with my kids the way I wanted to and the way they deserved. Instead of running around or playing actively, I found myself lying on the floor, the couch, the bed, or in the playroom, simply taking pictures.

This habit wasn't just about being physically tired; it was a clear symptom of giving all my energy to work and having none left for my family. These pictures, meant to capture moments of closeness, instead reflect a period where I was running on empty. My kids were getting a mom who was present in body but often too exhausted to be fully engaged.

Looking back, it baffles me how I let it get to that point. But recognizing this pattern was crucial—it was a clear sign that something had to change. This realization is one of the driving forces behind my business and this book. It's about finding a sustainable way to balance work and life, ensuring we have the energy to be present and active in the moments that truly matter with our loved ones.

Functioning Burnout Behavior

Checklist

Perhaps you have identified yourself in the stories above. Here is a checklist to help evaluate the different parts of your life. Check the boxes where you agree with the statements. At the end of this quick assessment, add up the number of boxes you've checked off to see where you fall within the spectrum of a functioning burnout.

Working Excessive Hours
☐ I regularly work late into the night or on weekends.
☐ I frequently take work home or am constantly available via email or phone.

Neglecting Personal Life
☐ I often prioritize work over personal relationships and leisure activities.

☐ I frequently miss family events, social gatherings, or personal milestones due to work commitments.

Perfectionism

☐ I set excessively high standards for myself and others.

☐ I micromanage tasks and am reluctant to delegate work to others.

Physical Presence

☐ I spend excessive time at the office or work-related events, arriving early and staying late.

☐ I take minimal or no vacation days, or work during vacations.

Overcommitment

☐ I often take on more projects and responsibilities than I can reasonably manage.

☐ I frequently volunteer for additional tasks or committees.

Technology Dependence

☐ I constantly check emails, messages, or work-related notifications, even during non-working hours.

☐ I bring work devices to social or family events.

Minimizing and Rationalizing

☐ I downplay the impact of my work habits on my health and relationships.

☐ I rationalize my behavior by highlighting the benefits of my hard work, such as career advancement or financial stability.

Avoiding Confrontation

☐ I steer conversations away from my work habits.

☐ I become defensive when questioned about my workload or work-life balance.

Health and Wellness

☐ I ignore or downplay physical and mental health issues caused by overworking, such as fatigue, stress or burnout.

☐ I engage in surface-level self-care activities to give the impression of balance.

Social Reinforcement

☐ I surround myself with other workaholics or people who reinforce my work habits.

☐ I praise or reward myself and others for excessive work.

Scoring
- Count the number of boxes you have checked.

  ○ 0–3: Low likelihood of functioning burnout tendencies.

  ○ 4–6: Moderate likelihood of functioning burnout tendencies; consider evaluating your work habits and their impact on your life.

  ○ 7–10: High likelihood of functioning burnout tendencies; it may be beneficial to seek strategies to balance your work and personal life or consult a professional for advice.

Burnout throughout the Years

About thirty years ago, burnout was a concept that existed quietly in the background, barely recognized, or understood. It first appeared with war veterans whose relentless experiences left them drained and weary. A couple of decades later, the word was attributed to caregivers, those selfless individuals tending to others' needs, and was called *caregiver burnout.* Fast-forward to the early 1990's, and burnout began to infiltrate the corporate world. Companies demanded long hours, and as technology advanced, the expectation to be constantly available and productive grew even more intense.

I first encountered burnout in my twenties, though I didn't have a name for it at the time. The term *burnout* hadn't yet entered mainstream vocabulary, especially not in the corporate context. Back then, it was just me and my husband, no family responsibilities to juggle, yet the weight of my obligations was crushing. This was my first experience with burnout, marked by an inability to recognize when to stop and take care of myself. Burnout shows up differently for everyone, but the common thread is a profound sense of depletion, a signal that something must change. My journey through burnout taught me the importance of self-awareness and the necessity of setting boundaries to protect my well-being.

This is how Capacity Creator® was born.

Chapter Two

Beyond Time Management: When Ignoring Capacity Leads to Burnout

The state of your capacity will determine the success of your commitments. — Melanie Sodka

Diary Entry

I don't even know where to begin today. I feel like I'm drowning again. I'm back in the same place I swore I'd never return to—burned out, frustrated, and lost. How could I let this happen again? It's like I've learned nothing from the first time. Instead of being smarter and stronger, I feel like a complete failure.

Work is an avalanche, and I'm buried so deep I can't see a way out. Every task feels insurmountable, and I'm terrified I'll collapse under the pressure. I'm too exhausted to catch up. How did I become this person again?

I'm embarrassed. I preach about managing stress, yet here I am, falling apart. I feel stupid for thinking I could handle everything, for ignoring my own advice. Who am I to teach others about balance when I can't find it myself?

I'm angry—angry at myself for letting it get this far, for not saying no, for always pushing and always falling short. I feel unworthy of success and happiness. Why can't I just get it right?

Part of me wants to give up, but I can't. There's too much at stake. People are counting on me. Yet, I feel so empty, so depleted. How do I balance everything when I can't keep myself together?

I need to find a way out of this darkness, but right now, it feels impossible. I'm scared I won't make it through this time. I don't want to let everyone down, but more than anything, I don't want to let myself down. Again.

The Difference Between Capacity and Time Management

Have you ever looked at your calendar and thought, *This should be manageable*, only to find yourself completely exhausted by the end of the day? Everything seems to fit neatly into a time slot, yet you still feel overwhelmed. Sound familiar?

From an early age, we were taught to view time as a finite resource—minutes attached to activities, tasks, or commitments. Whether someone told us how long something should take, or we estimated for ourselves, we've always used time as our primary measure of productivity. Meetings? Schedule them. Assignments? Write them down. An empty space on Tuesday at 2 p.m.? That meant we were free and could take on more. But there's a problem with this approach. We were never taught to account for the invisible factors. How long will it really take to get to that meeting? What if there's traffic? What if something goes wrong with the technology? These small, often forgotten details chip away at the time we thought we had.

If you feel constantly stretched thin or running late, it's not all on you. Our brains are wired to see an empty calendar space as available time. And, whether it's a work obligation or a social commitment, we feel compelled to fill that space. When someone asks if we're free, we glance at the calendar, see a gap, and say, "Sure, I can do that!" But when that packed day arrives, we realize we're booked solid and running on fumes. Day after day, this pattern repeats, and we wonder how long we can keep up this pace.

The truth is most of us are operating in a time deficit. Studies, like one from the *Harvard Business Review*, show that people tend to underestimate how long tasks will take—a phenomenon known as the *planning fallacy*. This leads to overcommitting and underdelivering, leaving us stressed, burned out, and constantly scrambling to keep up. This is where capacity management steps in. It's not just about managing time; it's about making sure we can actually handle everything we're committed to. Capacity management focuses on balancing our tasks and commitments with our available energy, skills, and resources. Instead of just packing our schedules with tasks, it helps us ensure we're not pushing past our limits.

Unlike time management, which is all about squeezing more into a schedule, capacity management is about sustainability. It helps us evaluate how much we can realistically take on without sacrificing our well-being. Capacity Management is designed to help you find that balance—not just to boost productivity, but to protect your energy and prevent burnout.

The result? A healthier, more sustainable way to approach both work and life, being productive without burning out, achieving more without sacrificing yourself in the process. Within the following chapters, you'll be introduced to tools that can help you master your capacity and take back control of your commitments.

Loving Your Career Won't Protect You from Burnout

In my thirties, I experienced my second bout of burnout, and it hit me in a completely different way. My schedule was packed, and I took pride in being a workaholic, always pushing myself to do more. Late nights were a norm, and I often sacrificed tucking my children into bed while reading bedtime stories, a choice that still haunts me.

This time, burnout wasn't just about feeling exhausted: it was my body's way of screaming for help. The symptoms were undeniable, and they forced me to confront the harsh reality that I was overextending myself once again. It became clear that loving what I did wasn't enough to protect me from burnout. I had to learn to balance my commitments, prioritize my well-being, and recognize the signs before they escalated. This experience taught me the crucial lesson that self-care is not a luxury but a necessity, especially when juggling multiple roles and responsibilities.

While contemplating my "repeat offender" behaviors, I discovered the concept of capacity. I no longer wanted to experience burnout and so I started to look at my own capacity and become curious about everyone else's around me. I was determined not to let burnout happen again and to help others who had to be experiencing the same thing in silence.

Capacity and prioritization are often confused, but they impact us in vastly different ways. Prioritization is about managing tasks—deciding what needs to get done and in what order. Capacity, though, is much bigger. It's about your whole self—your physical, mental, and emotional energy—and how well you're able to sustain it. Just like athletes need to pace themselves, protect their energy, and recover after exertion, we need to do the same to avoid burnout and stay effective. Capacity isn't just about checking things off a to-do list; it's about how well prepared we are, how we execute, and how we recover.

When we focus on capacity, we take a more holistic approach that goes beyond task management and annual goals, aligning our energy and resources to focus on the right things at the right time and ensuring we can fully engage in what matters most. Unlike prioritization, which zeroes in on tasks, capacity concerns the whole person—not only whether they are productive but also whether their activities are sustainable.

To help people better understand this balance, I developed a framework that highlights four states of capacity. It gives clarity on how we operate and helps us manage our commitments without stretching ourselves too thin. While time management is still essential—helping us organize and prioritize tasks—capacity management ensures that we have the energy and focus to manage those tasks effectively. Together, they help us work smarter, stay productive, and avoid burnout.

The Core Components of All Four States of Capacity

During the development of the Capacity Assessment tool, it was clear to me that no matter what state of capacity we are referring to, there are three core components: energy, purpose, and connection. Energy refers to the physical, emotional, and mental reserves we draw upon to complete tasks and navigate daily life. Purpose provides the direction and motivation behind our actions, giving meaning to the work we do and the goals we set. Connection involves the relationships and networks we maintain, which support us emotionally and practically, allowing us to share our experiences and collaborate with others. Together, these elements shape our overall capacity, determining how effectively we manage commitments and sustain a balanced life.

Paying attention to these components is essential for preventing burnout. When we neglect our energy levels by overcommitting or failing to rest, we deplete our ability to function at our best. Losing sight of our purpose can make tasks feel empty and unfulfilling, draining our motivation. A lack of meaningful connection can lead to isolation, increasing stress and reducing our resilience. By regularly assessing and nurturing our energy, purpose, and connection, we can better manage our capacity and protect ourselves from the exhaustion and overwhelm that lead to burnout.

Figure 2.1 illustrates the interplay between the three core components of capacity—Energy, Purpose, and Connection—intertwined with the four states of capacity: Maximized, Reserved, Indulgent, and Fatigued. While the focus here is on the essential components, the states of capacity, which we delve into in the next section, highlight the varying levels of balance and strain we experience as we manage our commitments and navigate life's demands.

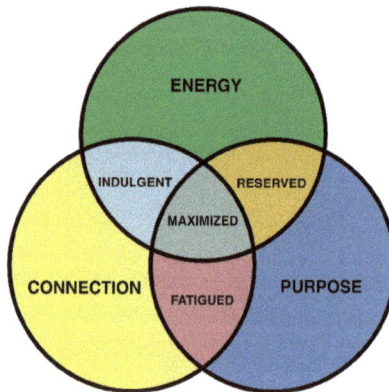

Figure 2.1. Core Components of Capacity

The **Purpose** component involves making decisions aligned with your values, leading to a sense of fulfillment. **Energy** is sustained when you maintain your mental, physical, and emotional well-being. A healthy ecosystem of friends, family, and colleagues ensures that you feel support and **Connection**.

Understanding the importance of energy, purpose, and connection in managing our capacity becomes even clearer when we look at real-life examples. Let me introduce you to two individuals, Rina and Gurdeep, whose experiences highlight how these core components play a critical role in preventing burnout. Through their stories, we'll explore how neglecting or nurturing these aspects of capacity can dramatically impact one's well-being and overall productivity.

Consider Grace, one of my clients, a project manager who meticulously plans her day down to the minute. Despite her detailed scheduling, she often finds herself running behind. The core component compromised in Grace's case is E*nergy*. While her calendar appears organized, it fails to account for the energy required to transition between tasks, manage mental fatigue from continuous focus, and manage unforeseen interruptions. This oversight leads to her feeling drained as her capacity is constantly stretched beyond its limits. Grace is operating in a *Fatigued* state of capacity, where her energy is depleted, making it difficult to perform tasks effectively. By failing to respect the natural ebbs and flows of her energy, she is overloading herself, leading to reduced productivity and increasing the risk of burnout. Recognizing and honoring her energy levels could help her manage her day more realistically, reducing the mental strain that comes with trying to do too much without proper breaks or recovery.

Similarly, Thomas, a software developer, carefully blocks out time for coding, meetings, and personal errands, yet frequently finds himself working late into the night. The core component compromised in Thomas' case is *Purpose*. While his time management skills are well structured, his capacity management suffers because he is not aligning his daily tasks with a clear sense of purpose or priority. He hasn't factored in the unpredictable nature of coding, such as debugging, unexpected client calls, or the cognitive load that comes with constant multitasking. Thomas is often operating in an *Indulgent* state of capacity, where he overextends himself without proper boundaries or purpose-driven prioritization. Although he excels at organizing his time, he hasn't set clear boundaries around what truly needs his focus or how to balance work demands with rest. This lack of purpose alignment creates a constant need to overwork, pulling him into long, unsustainable hours. By reassessing his purpose and determining what tasks are genuinely worth the extra time, he could better manage his capacity and reduce the frequency of late-night work, protecting himself from eventual burnout.

Which State of Capacity Are You In?

By recognizing which of the four states of capacity—Maximized, Reserved, Indulgent, or Fatigued—they're operating in, individuals can make better decisions and align their commitments with their well-being. When any of the three core components—Purpose, Energy, or Connection—are compromised, it can lead to different states of capacity. Take a moment to reflect on where you might currently find yourself:

- **Fatigued**: When energy is depleted, even if purpose and connection are intact. Individuals may feel aligned with their goals and supported but lack the energy to complete tasks.

  - **Here's what it may sound like**: "Despite still feeling connected to my purpose and the people around me, I am utterly exhausted. My energy is drained, and while my sense of meaning remains intact, the weight of fatigue makes it increasingly difficult to sustain my efforts and keep moving forward."

- **Indulgent**: When there is energy and connection but a disconnect from the purpose. Individuals may be busy and active but lack fulfillment and clarity on why they are doing what they do.

  - **Here's what it may sound like**: "I am taking on more than I should, enjoying the momentary satisfaction, but I feel a growing distance from my true purpose. While this extra load brings temporary fulfillment, my actions are increasingly misaligned with my deeper goals, leaving me feeling disconnected, overextended, and less grounded in what truly matters."

- **Reserved**: When there is energy and purpose, but a disconnection from the support system. Ambitious individuals in this state may neglect their social connections, reducing their resilience.

  - **Here's what it may sound like**: "I am fiercely pursuing my goals, driven by competition, yet my relationships feel neglected and disconnected. The lack of support and nurturing is starting to erode my resilience, making it harder to sustain the momentum behind my ambitious pursuits."

- **Maximized**: The ideal state where purpose, energy, and connection are all balanced and healthy, allowing individuals to function at their best.

  ○ **Here's what it may sound like**: "I am operating at full capacity, managing my commitments efficiently and making the most of my time and energy. However, I am keenly aware that this balance is fragile and could easily be disrupted if I don't carefully manage my energy, boundaries, and priorities."

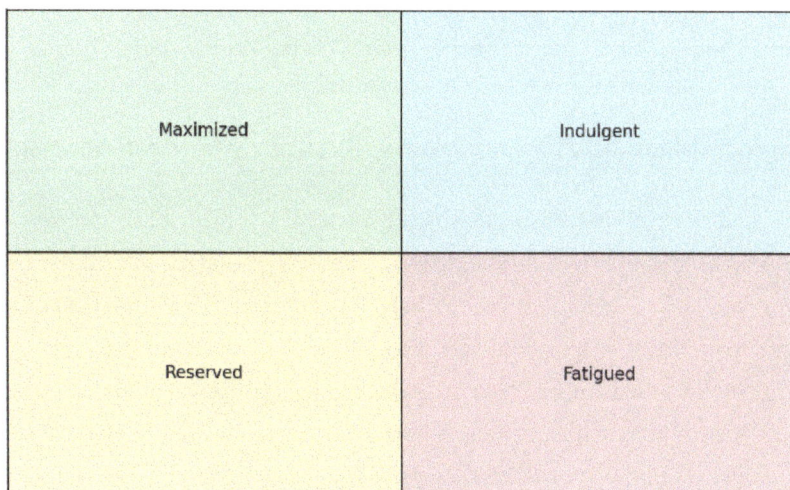

Maximized	Indulgent
Reserved	Fatigued

Figure 2.2. The Four States of Capacity

In today's fast-paced world, where the grind and hustle culture often dominate, it's easy to lose sight of our own limits. We push ourselves to the brink, juggling multiple commitments without realizing the toll it takes on our well-being. This is why I created the Four States of Capacity framework—a simple, intuitive system designed to help both individuals and organizations quickly assess their current capacity and find their way back to balance.

The beauty of this framework (Figure 2.2) lies in its accessibility. There's no need for complex manuals or lengthy instructions; these capacity tools are crafted to seamlessly integrate into your daily routine. Whether you're at home or work, understanding your capacity state allows you to make better decisions about how to allocate your time and energy. You're not just planning tasks; you're honoring your physical, mental, and emotional boundaries.

Managing your capacity means recognizing when you're operating at full steam, when you need to reserve energy, or when it's time to recharge. By tuning into these states, you can create a sustainable balance that supports both your personal life and your professional goals. This framework empowers you to navigate life with greater awareness, helping you thrive without burning out.

So, instead of constantly pushing yourself to do more, take a step back and assess where you stand. The Four States of Capacity framework provides the practical tools you need to find a rhythm that works for you, making it easier to achieve your goals without sacrificing your well-being.

Overcommitment: A Functioning Burnout's Hottest Accessory

Work had become my passion, or so it seemed. With no kids, minimal responsibilities, a supportive husband, and a few key monetary incentives, I was driven to keep up a relentless pace. There was nothing to hold me back. Once I found my stride, I was unstoppable. I transformed from an assistant marketing manager who relied on her boss to make the tough decisions into a training and development manager leading an international project that would have cost the company hundreds of thousands of dollars to develop and execute. It was one of the most exhilarating projects of my life. I worked furiously on planes, in airports, and in the office until late at night. I'd come home, catch up briefly with my husband, and then we'd go to bed. I'd wake up thinking about my projects and the endless possibilities. Lather, rinse, repeat.

I was the first in my family to hold a high-paying management position in a prominent packaged goods company. This was a source of immense pride for my parents and impressive for a small-town girl like me. With a BA in sociology and a postgraduate certificate in human resources management, I felt accomplished, but it wasn't enough. So, I embarked on an MBA full-time while continuing to work full-time as well. After all, I had a lot of capacity, and no one was telling me to slow down. The cycle continued.

Then we were blessed with a pregnancy.

I hate to admit this, but in the spirit of full transparency, I share these thoughts to reach others in similar situations: I was pregnant and excited, but I couldn't help but worry about how this would impact my career. I was on an exhilarating trajectory, potentially moving to headquarters and then across the ocean. That was the ultimate fuel for my relentless ambition. But how would a baby and a pregnancy leave fit into these plans?

I felt selfish and irresponsible for having these thoughts, but I had worked consecutive years of long hours and given myself entirely to the company. How could I walk away for a year? What would this do to my career? I feared this tiny unborn being would revoke any possibility of moving forward. I told no one of these thoughts and feelings. I was ashamed and conflicted. Despite loving being pregnant, I kept up with my projects during the nine months and even graduated with my MBA at the end of my first trimester.

When the baby arrived, I realized I had no idea how to stop working, how to sit still, how to watch a sleeping baby, how to function on little sleep, or how to disconnect from work completely. I know many women yearn for this time, but I was unprepared for the stillness, the slowing down, the "enjoy every moment" mindset. I realized I was truly addicted to work and the adrenaline it gave me. Years later, I understood that the adrenaline drip was prescribed by corporations that knew exactly how to leverage a person with high capacity who would deprioritize wellness and balance.

I took my maternity leave, came back a little early, and at fifty percent work reduction. I stayed for six months and then handed in my resignation letter. I had decided that this pace was no longer sustainable. I had to make choices for my new little family.

Burnout has become the hottest accessory in today's high-paced, achievement-oriented culture. Much like a designer handbag or the latest tech gadget, flaunting one's exhaustion is often seen as signaling dedication, hard work, and success. This pervasive mindset glorifies relentless hustle and self-sacrifice, equating constant busyness with value and worth. However, beneath this facade lies a detrimental reality: burnout is not a trendy emblem of success but a serious and harmful consequence of chronic stress and overcommitment. By normalizing and even celebrating burnout, we perpetuate a cycle of unsustainable living that undermines our well-being and productivity.

In her book *The Burnout Fix*, Dr. Jacinta M. Jiménez points out the top myths associated with burnout, one of them being that "burnout is increasing because we're just not as tough as we used to be." According to Jiménez, research reveals that when demands from our work and our capacities as humans become mismatched, they can lead to burnout.

Five Myths about Burnout I Used to Believe

1. Burnout is the cost of ambition.

2. Burnout is normal and it's ok to suffer from at least one.

3. Burnout happens to those who can't prioritize well.

4. Burnout is a badge of honor.

5. Burnout means you can finally take a rest.

Now that we've busted some myths about burnout, let's talk about something that often fuels these misconceptions: toxic positivity. It's that pressure to stay upbeat and keep smiling, even when things are tough. This kind of thinking can make us ignore our real struggles, slapping on a happy face instead of dealing with what's really going on.

Toxic positivity is the overgeneralization of a happy, optimistic state across all situations. It pressures individuals to maintain positivity even in the face of adversity, leading to a suppression of genuine emotions and an invalidation of real experiences. In many ways, this toxic mindset feeds directly into the burnout myths we've just explored. The belief that "burnout is normal and it's okay to suffer from at least one" is often fueled by the same culture that insists we keep smiling and "powering through," no matter how depleted we feel.

But here's where capacity management becomes crucial. By recognizing and respecting our emotional, physical, and mental limits, we can start dismantling these myths and the toxic positivity that reinforces them. Capacity management empowers us to acknowledge when we are stretched too thin, to admit when we are struggling, and to seek balance rather than succumb to the false narrative that relentless positivity or ambition is the only acceptable path.

Toxic positivity intersects with our understanding of burnout and how embracing a more balanced approach to our capacity can help us combat both pervasive issues. This was fascinating for my capacity research because it fueled my curiosity about toxic positivity and time shaming, which wreak havoc on our mental health. It's like being stuck with an overly enthusiastic cheerleader and a stern clock-watcher who are constantly at odds, leaving you to navigate a maze of unrealistic expectations and guilt. This guarantees mental exhaustion, as you try to smile through the stress and squeeze productivity out of every fleeting moment.

I've personally often felt the pressure to put on a brave face, as if showing anything less than 'OK' somehow makes me less capable. Over time, I realized that constantly pretending to be fine can make you believe there's something wrong with you for feeling overwhelmed or distressed. It's easy to internalize those emotions and start to think you're not strong enough or that you're somehow flawed for struggling. Not everyone copes with stress by getting busy. For many, these messages are harmful, leading to increased feelings of depression and anxiety.

Healthy Capacity Audit

Auditing the health of your capacity involves evaluating your management of purpose, energy, and connection. Use this audit to reflect on these areas and identify potential improvements to prevent burnout.

Purpose
1. *Clarity and Motivation*

   - Do I have a clear sense of purpose in my work and personal life?

   - Do I feel motivated by my goals and objectives?

   - Am I focusing on what truly matters to me?

2. *Alignment with Values*

- Is my work aligned with my personal values and goals?

- Do I feel a sense of fulfillment in my daily activities?

- Is my work engaging and less stressful because it aligns with my values?

Energy
1. *Balanced Workload*

- Am I aware of my personal limits and managing my workload accordingly?

- Do I often feel chronically stressed or physically exhausted?

- Have I balanced my tasks to avoid burnout?

2. *Rest and Recovery*

- Do I prioritize activities that restore my energy, such as adequate sleep and regular exercise?

- Do I engage in leisure activities that help me relax and recover?

- Am I maintaining my physical and mental health to manage work demands effectively?

3. *Healthy Boundaries*

- Have I set boundaries to protect my time and energy from excessive work demands?

- Am I comfortable saying no when necessary?

- Do I delegate tasks to manage my workload better?

Connection

1. *Social Support*

   - Do I have strong social connections at work and in my personal life?

   - Do I feel a sense of belonging and emotional support from my relationships?

   - Can I rely on my social network to buffer against stress?

2. *Collaboration and Teamwork*

   - Are my relationships with colleagues positive and collaborative?

   - Do I feel part of a supportive team that enhances my job satisfaction?

   - Does effective teamwork reduce feelings of isolation and stress for me?

3. *Communication*

   - Do I communicate openly and honestly with colleagues and supervisors about my workload and stressors?

   - Am I proactive in discussing my support needs?

   - Do I feel comfortable addressing issues before they lead to burnout?

Reflection and Action Plan

- **Purpose:** Identify any areas where your sense of purpose could be clearer or better aligned with your values. Set specific goals to enhance clarity and motivation.

- **Energy:** Evaluate your workload, rest, recovery, and boundaries. Implement changes to balance your energy and prevent burnout.

- **Connection:** Strengthen your social support, improve collaboration and teamwork, and enhance communication to foster a supportive work environment.

Use this audit regularly to monitor your capacity and adjust as needed to maintain a healthy balance.

The Unexpected Return

Working with corporations has given me such pride and pleasure in helping others have difficult conversations about overwhelm, capacity management, and burnout prevention. It was a surreal moment when I was called back to the very corporation where I had once worked and ultimately left burned out. Ten years had passed, and now they wanted me to create a proposal to be their keynote speaker for a professional development day. The VP of marketing from my time there had risen to the position of president. We had always been on good terms, so I wasn't entirely surprised when he reached out.

I prepared my proposal meticulously, focusing on capacity management and meaningful conversations about workplace stress. When the day came to present it, I felt a mix of nostalgia and anticipation. As I stepped into the familiar boardroom, memories of late nights and endless meetings came flooding back. The president, now an older yet still very familiar version of his former self, greeted me warmly.

We dove into the proposal, and I could see his brow furrow as he read through my recommendations. Then, as if on cue, he blurted out, "You're going to teach people to say no? We can't have that. We need people to work!"

Ah, there it was—the reaction I had anticipated. I couldn't help but smile.

"Charles," I began, leaning in slightly, "it's not about teaching people to say no. It's about teaching them to say yes to the right things." He looked at me, clearly puzzled. "I help people have meaningful conversations about their stress levels associated with work. I provide them with tools to communicate these issues effectively with their managers. It's about improving productivity and well-being, not about shutting down work."

He sat back, considering my words. "So, you're saying it's about prioritizing and managing capacity, not just cutting down on tasks?"

"Exactly," I replied. "It's about creating a sustainable work environment where people can thrive. When employees feel understood and supported, they're more engaged and productive."

He nodded slowly, a hint of a smile creeping onto his face. "Alright, let's give it a shot."

And just like that, I found myself in the position of helping the very company that had once burned me out, now committed to fostering a healthier, more balanced workplace. The irony wasn't lost on me, and it felt good to be back on my own terms, armed with the tools to make a real difference.

Side note: The session went extremely well, but I couldn't help noticing how tethered one of the directors was to his device—frequently leaving from the back of the room, taking calls, and responding to messages, while his team sat trying to focus and absorb messages from my keynote about capacity management, which included distraction management.

Chapter Three

Defining Distraction, Destruction, and Avoidance

Time management is pain management. Distractions cost us time, and like all actions, they are spurred by the desire to escape discomfort. — Nir Eyal

Diary Entry

*D*ear distraction—disguised as opportunity,

Since I've known you, I have become an opportunistic multitasking adrenaline junkie. I have always loved you, but I get too absorbed by you. When you show up, it's a race to the finish line to reach you. I start out fast and my finish is lackluster.

You make me insatiable. Your adrenaline is the best out there. Your temporary payoffs keep me hooked. But the aftermath is ugly. The crash is too sacrificial, and I no longer want your highs.

I need to resign from you and your conniving ways. You do not serve my deepest needs, and you steal joy from the present day.

I can't do this anymore. I need to be more disciplined and discerning. If you wave at me, I shall ignore you and carry on. Please don't take offense.

Actually, I don't care if you take offense. You are my greatest offense.

Proudly,

The newly resigned me

The Most Distracted We've Ever Been

Ever feel like you're living in a whirlwind of distractions? You're not alone. Studies by Gloria Mark and others show that we get pulled away from what we're doing every three minutes! And it takes a whopping twenty-three minutes to get back on track after each interruption. We're constantly glued to our phones, tapping, and swiping on average over 3,500 times a day, according to a report by Dscout. No wonder we're always feeling rushed and overwhelmed!

But here's the thing: instead of wishing for more time, what if we focused on something deeper?

Capacity is not just about managing minutes and hours—it's about having the energy and passion to do what really matters. So instead of saying, "I wish I had more time," try saying, "I want to create capacity." It's a game-changer.

Let's talk about the big issue: distractions. We've all fallen into the multitasking trap, believing it makes us more efficient. But here's the truth: multitasking is actually making us less intelligent. It's similar to pulling an all-nighter and then trying to operate heavy machinery the next day. And notifications? They're like mini stress bombs, constantly triggering our cortisol levels and putting our health at risk. These interruptions drain our focus, impair our productivity, and leave us feeling more scattered and stressed than ever.

Here are some eye-opening statistics that highlight how distracted we are today:

1. **Screen Time:** Adults in the US spend an average of three hours and forty-three minutes on their mobile devices daily (source: He).

2. **Social Media Addiction:** Social media users spend an average of two hours and twenty-four minutes per day on social platforms (source: GWI).

3. **Workplace Productivity:** Multitasking can reduce productivity by as much as forty percent (source: American Psychological Association).

4. **Focus and Attention:** The average attention span has dropped from twelve seconds in the year 2000 to just eight seconds today shorter than

that of a goldfish, which is nine seconds (source: Microsoft Canada).

5. **Notification Overload:** The average person receives around 63.5 notifications per day on their smartphone (source: Pielot et al.).

6. **Mental Health:** Excessive smartphone use has been linked to increased stress, anxiety, and depression. About fifty percent of teens report feeling addicted to their mobile devices (source: Common Sense).

These statistics paint a clear picture: we are more distracted than ever, and it's taking a toll on our productivity, mental health, and overall well-being.

The Addiction to Distraction: How It's Eroding Our Capacity

People are hungrier for recognition more than they are for food and it's a stark reality of our modern lives. We are addicted to the notifications on our devices, and this addiction is making us sick. The anticipation of a response can be stressful. Unwritten rules, like not leaving someone "on read"—where the sender can see that you've read their message without immediately replying—are highly distracting. The average response time is now just thirty minutes when returning a text, and we send and receive over a hundred texts a day on average. You can do the math. How is this even possible?

We are feeding this desire for recognition with an "all-access" pass to social media channels. We can't ignore the flashing lights, the vibrations, the dings, and pings. It's primal. It's like someone tapping you on the shoulder from behind—your instinct is to turn around and assess whether to run or fight.

There is no handbook, no formal "dos and don'ts" for navigating social media. There are no instructions on how to participate, no rulebook or etiquette training. We are just given the tools to promote ourselves, our beliefs, our thoughts, and our ideas. But what's the return? A dopamine hit each time someone likes or responds and as the viewership continues to rise. Consequently, we are flooding our bodies with elevated stress hormones and increased cortisol levels.

In my TEDx talk, I delved deeper into this addiction to distraction. I explained how our constant need for recognition and validation through social media and other digital platforms is eroding our capacity to focus, work effectively, and maintain healthy relationships. We are constantly pulled away from our tasks, our goals, and even our loved ones by the lure of our devices.

This addiction isn't just a minor inconvenience; it's a significant threat to our well-being. The stress induced by our need for constant connectivity can lead to burnout, anxiety, and other health issues. The irony is that while we seek recognition and connection through our devices, we are often left feeling more isolated and stressed.

Understanding this addiction to distraction is crucial for reclaiming our capacity. We need to set boundaries with our devices, practice mindfulness, and prioritize real, meaningful connections over digital validation. By doing so, we can start to rebuild our capacity, reduce stress, and live healthier, more fulfilling lives.

In today's fast-paced world, the lines between distraction and addiction often blur, leading to a common misconception that they are one and the same. However, it's crucial to understand that while both can impact our productivity and well-being, they are fundamentally different. Distraction is often a temporary diversion that pulls us away from our tasks and goals, whereas addiction is a deeper, more ingrained compulsion that can significantly alter our behavior and life choices. Understanding this distinction is essential as we navigate the complexities of modern life. Distractions can typically be managed with strategies to improve focus and time management. However, addiction requires a more profound level of intervention and support. The trend of using these terms interchangeably can dilute the seriousness of addiction, undermining the real psychological and physical impact it has on individuals.

To illustrate this, let me share a story about someone who found themself caught in unhealthy habits, leading them to a profound realization about their psychological safety needs. This journey highlights the importance of addressing these habits with the attention they deserve, ensuring that those affected receive the necessary support and understanding to find their path to well-being.

Addiction, Distraction, and Psychological Safety: Navigating the Boundaries Between Compulsion and Healthy Diversion

Benjamin is a family friend. He is a spirited ten-year-old who finds solace and excitement in the world of gaming. Benjamin, much like many young gamers, immerses himself in gaming after school and into the late hours of the night, much to his parents' chagrin. Despite their efforts to pry him away from the screen, Robbie's devotion to gaming remains unwavering.

Concerned about his seemingly compulsive or addictive gaming habits, his parents turn to a psychologist for guidance. To their surprise, the psychologist's assessment unveils a different narrative: Benjamin isn't addicted to gaming per se; rather, he's grappling with deeper issues. It turns out that Benjamin's struggles extend beyond the realm of gaming consoles. His difficulties at school, particularly with a less-than-supportive teacher, have left him feeling inadequate and intellectually inferior. Moreover, his social circle is sparse, leaving him isolated and disconnected from his peers. Adding to his woes, Benjamin feels stifled by the typical lack of autonomy for someone his age. What becomes evident through this examination is the crucial role of psychological safety in Benjamin's life. The psychologist identifies three fundamental psychological needs that gaming fulfills for Benjamin, shedding light on their importance beyond the digital realm.

First, gaming provides Benjamin with a sense of confidence. Conquering levels and achieving milestones in games boost his self-esteem, serving as a stark contrast to his experiences in the real world. Second, gaming offers him a platform for social interaction, albeit virtual. Through gaming, Benjamin finds companionship and validation, through a headset rather than in face-to-face interactions. And third, gaming grants Benjamin a degree of autonomy rarely experienced elsewhere in his life. The ability to make decisions and chart his course within the game world empowers him in ways that are lacking in his everyday existence.

This narrative of Benjamin's journey highlights a broader truth: when individuals' psychological needs are unmet, they seek fulfillment elsewhere, often leading to disengagement or dependency on external stimuli. As we reflect on

Benjamin's story, let us consider how we can foster psychological safety within our own interactions with those around us. By recognizing and addressing the core psychological needs of confidence, connection, and autonomy, we can create spaces where individuals feel valued, supported, and empowered to thrive. This applies not only to children but to adults as well. When we feel disconnected and distracted, we seek to avoid this discomfort and find ways to fill the void.

How These Behaviors Show up During Burnout

In my first bout of burnout during my twenties, when I was working in the corporate world, I didn't fully realize how miserable I was. I had some wonderful leaders, managers, and allies, but there were also a few individuals who made my work life atrocious and practically unendurable. Because my background was in sociology and HR, adjusting to a corporate environment was a steep learning curve. I grew up quickly at this organization and achieved a lot of success, but it came at a significant cost.

When things were bad—when I lacked confidence, was constantly challenged, rarely appreciated, and always under stress—I would self-sabotage. The form this took was shopping. Shopping became my tool for quick fixes of happiness and moments of forgetting about everything. Each purchase gave me a brief sense of delight and escape, but this was short-lived. The euphoria would fade as soon as the credit card bill arrived, often exceeding what I had in my bank account. These self-sabotaging shopping habits continued for several years. I knew it was a problem. I constantly tried to rejig my finances, figuring out ways to pay off my mounting debts. Eventually, I did manage to pay them off, but not without enduring years of financial stress and emotional turmoil.

I used shopping to numb the feelings of discontentment and stress at work. The search for dopamine and those fleeting moments of happiness from buying something new became an addiction, even though I knew deep down I couldn't afford it. It was my way of masking the pain and frustration of my job. While others might be prone to substance abuse, eating disorders, or other means to numb themselves, I chose shopping and spending.

Reflecting on this in therapy has been a revelation. I would never have admitted these behaviors five years after quitting my corporate job. Therapy has allowed me to acknowledge and understand these patterns. When I feel discontented or lack confidence, I now recognize my self-sabotaging tendencies. It's important for all of us to identify how we deal with such feelings and to seek healthier ways to cope. Therapy has been a blessing, helping me confront these issues and find better ways to manage my emotions and stress.

The World of Pills, Potions, and Unsolicited Advice

When our endocrine system is disrupted, our digestion is off, or our hormones are out of balance, we immediately eliminate something from our diet. We say no to these irritants so we can say yes to feeling better. We have apps to track our steps, calories, and even our sleep cycles. We're on a first-name basis with our pharmacist and have enough vitamins to start a small business.

However, we are generally not as attentive to our capacity and mental health. When we overconsume food, we don't feel well, and when we overindulge in commitments, we feel bloated with obligations. Our capacity gives us the same signals, but unlike for food, when it comes to work and other areas of our lives, we are less likely to cut anything out and say no.

Imagine this: you've just had a slightly suspicious-looking cupcake and suddenly feel a tickle in your throat. Panic ensues! You rush to your medicine cabinet, which looks like a mini pharmacy. There are pills for digestion, potions for detoxing, and sprays for soothing that tickly throat. Not to mention, your well-meaning neighbor is always ready with unsolicited advice about the latest superfood or miracle cure. "Have you tried kale-infused coconut water? It's life-changing!"

We are bombarded with health tips from every direction. "Avoid gluten, dairy, sugar, air, and happiness!" The sheer number of dietary restrictions and newly marketed illnesses are enough to make anyone's head spin. Yet, we follow these tips, popping probiotics like candy and drinking enough herbal tea to float a small boat.

In our quest for optimal health, we often forget to listen to our own bodies and needs. Instead of being driven by the latest trends and fads, we should strive to cultivate a balanced and intuitive approach to our well-being. After all, true health is not about adhering to rigid rules but about finding what genuinely nourishes and sustains us, both physically and mentally. By tuning into our own unique rhythms and embracing a holistic perspective, we can achieve a state of well-being that is both sustainable and fulfilling.

We treat the pains from surpassing our capacity differently. Instead of saying no, we push through. We squeeze things in. Our capacity is giving us warning signs of breakdown just as our physical system does, but it's not just a bellyache, fatigue, or rash—it's burnout.

Imagine if we treated our mental health like our physical health. Picture a mental health cabinet filled with affirmations, mindfulness apps, and stress balls. Your friend calls you up, "Have you tried the latest self-care routine? It's all the rage!" There'd be trendy stress detox diets where you eliminate one stressor a week. "Sorry, I can't answer emails this week—I'm on a strict mental wellness regimen!"

We need to start treating our mental and emotional health with the same care and attention we give to our physical health. Recognize the signs of overcapacity—stress, anxiety, burnout—and take proactive steps to eliminate the irritants. Say no to unnecessary commitments, seek support, and prioritize your mental wellness. Just as we would with any physical ailment, we need to be diligent and proactive in maintaining our mental and emotional health. So, let's stock up our mental health cabinet and say cheers to a balanced, healthy life!

Quick Fixes—A Booming Economy

Ah, the human quest for quick fixes—an adventure more thrilling than a treasure hunt and sometimes as futile as trying to catch your shadow. Picture this: our ancient ancestors, the prehistoric humans, facing a sabre-toothed tiger. Their trusty reptilian brains screamed, *Run! Hide! Do anything to escape this beast!* Fast-forward a few millennia, and while the sabre-toothed tigers have thankfully disappeared, our instinct to flee from discomfort remains hilariously intact.

Today's modern sabre-toothed tigers? Stress, anxiety, and the looming deadline of that report you haven't started yet. Enter the Anxiety Economy, a bustling marketplace filled with magical potions (also known as supplements), enchanted gadgets (wellness tech), and mystical scrolls (self-help books) promising instant relief. Our reptilian brains, still wired to avoid harm at all costs, leap at these shiny quick fixes. Instead of battling with rocks and sticks, we now combat our stress with an ever-expanding arsenal of anxiety-busting products. Got stress? There's an app for that! Feeling anxious? Pop this pill! Overwhelmed? How about a meditation course that promises enlightenment in just five days? We swipe our credit cards and tap Buy Now like a caveman wielding his club, all in the name of defeating the relentless beast of boredom.

But here's the twist in our epic saga: these quick fixes often act like the mythical Hydra—cut off one head (or stressor) and two more grow in its place. Each new purchase, while offering a brief respite, often leads to a new layer of complexity and, ironically, more stress. The subscription to the meditation app becomes another reminder on your phone, the supplements clutter your nightstand, and the self-help books pile up, unread, on your shelf.

So, we end up in this comical cycle: our reptilian brain yells at us again. *Quick, do something!* We buy into an even newer and even quicker fix, experience that fleeting relief again, but our stress doesn't disappear—it's just temporarily masked. Our wallets are lighter, but our stress is just as high. In this grand theater of human behavior, the irony is both amusing and poignant. Maybe, just maybe, the real solution is to slow down, face our dragons head-on, and avoid the shiny promises of the Anxiety Economy.

Here are some examples of clients who acted:

1. **Leah's Meditation App:** Leah, a young professional, spent hundreds of dollars on various meditation apps and online courses to manage her anxiety. While these tools provided temporary relief, her underlying stress from overwork and lack of work-life balance remained unaddressed. It wasn't until she sought comprehensive therapy that she began to see long-term improvement.

2. **Steven's Supplement Regimen:** Steven turned to a range of supplements advertised as natural anxiety cures. Despite spending significant amounts of money, he found no noticeable improvement in his anxiety levels. Eventually, he realized that lifestyle changes and professional counseling were more effective than the supplements he had been relying on.

3. **Carson's Wellness Gadgets:** Carson invested in several high-tech well-

ness gadgets, including a stress-tracking wearable and a light-therapy lamp. While these provided some benefits, they did not tackle his main stressor: a toxic work environment. It took a career change for Carson to experience a meaningful reduction in his anxiety.

The Anxiety Economy, while filled with products and services aimed at relieving stress and anxiety, often focuses on short-term fixes rather than addressing the root causes of these issues. Individuals spend significant money without achieving lasting relief. Understanding the limitations of these solutions and seeking comprehensive, long-term strategies for mental health are crucial for true well-being.

This table summarizes the numbing behaviors and coping mechanisms that people use to avoid dealing with stress, anxiety, pain, or discomfort, and the reasons why people may turn to them.

Behavior	Examples	Reasons
Substance Abuse	Alcohol, drugs, prescription medication misuse	Escape reality, alleviate stress or anxiety, temporarily improve mood
Overeating	Binge eating, emotional eating, eating junk food	Source of comfort, distraction from emotional pain, dopamine release creating temporary pleasure
Excessive Screen Time	Binge-watching TV shows or movies, excessive gaming, mindless scrolling on social media	Easy escape from real-life problems, immersive distraction from emotions or stressors
Compulsive Shopping	Shopping sprees, online shopping, buying unnecessary items	Quick dopamine hit, sense of control or accomplishment, momentarily forget problems
Workaholism	Working excessively long hours, taking on extra projects, neglecting personal life for work	Avoid personal issues, gain sense of purpose and productivity, mask feelings of inadequacy
Gambling	Casino gambling, online betting, lottery tickets	Thrill and excitement, possibility of winning big, form of escape
Excessive Exercise	Overtraining, compulsive gym visits, pushing physical limits	Release endorphins, temporary mood improvement, sense of achievement, avoid emotional issues
Self-Harm	Cutting, burning, other forms of self-injury	Physical pain as a distraction from emotional pain, feeling something tangible when feeling numb
Over-socializing	Constantly going out, filling every moment with social activities, never being alone	Distraction from personal issues, prevent sitting with thoughts, sense of belonging and validation
Engaging in Risky Behaviors	Reckless driving, unsafe sexual practices, extreme sports	Adrenaline rush, temporary high, rebellion against feeling trapped or controlled by problems

Table 3.1. Behaviors by People to Avoid Stress and Anxiety

Reflection: have you adopted any of these behaviors during times of stress or anxiety? If so, take a moment to think about it and even capture a few thoughts.

Navigating the Triple Threat: Distraction, Destruction, and Avoidance

In the realm of capacity management, particularly within frameworks like Ego-cake® (which will be shared in chapter 11), understanding the nuances between distraction, destruction, and avoidance is paramount. *Distraction*, in essence, is the interruption of focus and attention by both external and internal stimuli, leading to diminished productivity and efficiency. External distractions include notifications, social media, emails, and interruptions from colleagues or family, all of which disrupt workflow and concentration. Internal distractions, on the other hand, involve personal thoughts, worries, and daydreams that divert mental energy from tasks. The symptoms of distraction include frequent task-switching, an inability to complete tasks, procrastination, and feeling overwhelmed by numerous pending tasks. Effective management strategies for distraction involve setting boundaries, creating a focused work environment, employing techniques such as Pomodoro Effect, named after the Pomodoro Technique, which is a productivity method that uses short, timed intervals (usually 25 minutes, called "Pomodoros") of focused work followed by a brief break. This cycle helps to maintain concentration, reduce mental fatigue, and break large tasks into manageable chunks. The technique promotes sustained focus, minimizes distractions, and enhances productivity by creating a sense of urgency within each timed interval. This technique and others, are engaging in mindfulness practices to enhance concentration.

Destruction, conversely, refers to the deliberate or inadvertent breakdown of one's mental, emotional, or physical resources, leading to a significant decline in overall capacity. This can manifest mentally through continuous negative self-talk, exposure to toxic environments, or overwhelming workloads; emotionally through unresolved conflicts, persistent stress, and lack of support; and physically through neglect of health via poor diet, lack of exercise, and insufficient rest. Symptoms of destruction include chronic stress, burnout, anxiety, depression, and physical health issues such as fatigue and illness. To counteract these effects, strategies such as implementing self-care routines, seeking professional help, building supportive relationships, and establishing healthy work-life boundaries are essential.

Avoidance is the deliberate evasion of tasks, responsibilities, or situations perceived as stressful or challenging. It leads to procrastination, increased stress, and a sense of guilt or shame. Effective management of avoidance includes breaking tasks into manageable steps, developing stress-coping strategies, utilizing accountability partners, and employing cognitive-behavioral techniques.

By recognizing and addressing distraction, destruction, and avoidance, individuals can better manage their capacity, maintain focus, and sustain their well-being in both professional and personal spheres.

Chapter Four

Understanding How Your Personality Influences Bandwidth

Understanding your personality is essential to managing your capacity, allowing you to align your energy and resources with your true self. — Anonymous

Diary Entry

I just got back from a work function, and all I can think about is how out of place I felt. We did that personality test, the one where everyone gets categorized into these neat little boxes. Of course, the results dominated the conversation for the rest of the evening.

My results? Double amiable. Yep, the friendly one. The one who's good at making people feel comfortable but apparently not much else.

Everyone else's results? Dominating, leading, concise, decision-makers. All the qualities you'd expect from Ivy League business grads in a packaged goods company.

I felt like an imposter the entire time. Sitting there, listening to everyone else talk about their results with pride and confidence, while I tried to muster a smile. Friendly. Who wants to be the friendly one in a room full of leaders and decision-makers? It's like I'm the odd one out, the one who doesn't belong.

I'm embarrassed. Mortified, really. I wanted to crawl under the table and hide when they announced my results. How do I compete in this environment when my biggest strength is being friendly? It feels so trivial, so insignificant compared to what they bring to the table.

No one wants the friendly one. They want leaders, movers, shakers. People who get things done, who make decisions, who lead with authority. And then there's me, just trying to keep everyone happy, trying to be liked. It feels so small, so unimportant.

Is Our Capacity Influenced by Our Personality Style?

Understanding the interplay between distraction, destruction, and avoidance lays the groundwork for deeper exploration into how our personalities further influence overall capacity. Personality traits significantly shape how we manage distractions, cope with potential destruction, and confront or avoid challenges. Whether someone is naturally predisposed to high empathy, perfectionism, or idealism, these traits can either enhance their resilience and focus or exacerbate their vulnerability to capacity depletion. Recognizing and adapting to these inherent personality traits allow for more tailored and effective strategies in capacity management, ultimately fostering a balanced and sustainable approach to personal and professional commitments.

Awarded for My Overly Ambitious Nature

It was the annual end-of-year conference. Bright sunlight streamed in from the floor-to-ceiling windows of the auditorium that faced the deer-sighting ravine. People filed in and helped themselves to hors d'oeuvres and a slice of the jumbo branded corporate cake, meticulously sliced into one hundred equal pieces.

The room was set up with balloons bobbing to the beat of high-energy dance music pumping through large speakers anchored on either side of the stage. The awards table, decorated with beautiful glass trophies, awaited the moment when they would be handed out to the nominated, worthy employees. These awards were prestigious and highly sought after; winning one meant your career was set, your name etched in the company's history.

People took their seats in anticipation of the awards presentation. The music lowered, voices hushed to a quiet, and the president took to the mic. A humorous and engaging man, he broke the tension with a few jokes and soft jabs at his usual suspects on the leadership team, his close colleagues. Executives were called up to read the nomination scripts and present the awards. Pictures were taken, rounds of applause were given. The room grew quiet as the last award was about to be read. This was the big one: the President's Award.

The executive started to read the nomination submission aloud: "This nominee is known for her stretch goals, which she reaches every single year. She is admired by her team and those across the organization. Her tenacious approach to getting results and exceeding them is unlike any other. She is dedicated to her work and negotiates the best deals...."

Now, this was looking great! This woman knows how to get things done!

The nomination script continued. "She is the first to arrive, last to leave, and sacrifices family time to be here as long as it takes. She sits on many committees, has chaired our annual fundraising initiatives, mentors many new team members, volunteers on the breakfast club committee.... She sacrifices family time for this company...."

The script seemed to go on for hours. Who could this woman be? Isn't she amazing? How does she do it all? Can't we all be like that?

"And this year's recipient of the President's Award goes to ..." and they called my name. Elated, excited, grateful—those were only some of the feelings coursing through my body. My career was set. All that hard work had paid off. I could now ...

I could now what? Do more? Be more? Volunteer more?

One year later, I left the company. I was burned out and had no idea how I was going to top that performance. Two months later, after I left the company, my husband said, "I got my wife back."

Was this the moment that everyone was gunning for? This awful description was the prestige and acknowledgment people worked for. How many of you are successful because of the hustle, the hours, the all-nighters, your competitive nature, your win-at-all-costs mindset, and your fierce negotiating tactics?

As a former HR professional, I often found myself questioning whether our hiring practices are unknowingly steeped in hustle culture, particularly through the interview process. Commonly asked questions such as, "Tell us about a big stretch goal and how you achieved it" or "Describe how you managed a tight deadline" subtly reinforce the glorification of relentless productivity and the expectation of overextending oneself. These prompts don't just assess a candidate's capability; they implicitly prioritize those who are willing to go above and beyond, often at the expense of their personal well-being. Even hypothetical questions like "How would you design a spaceship to get to the moon in forty-five minutes?" signal that extreme, and often unrealistic achievements are valued over sustainable effort and long-term growth.

These kinds of questions may unintentionally vet candidates based on their tolerance for high pressure and overload, rather than fostering a culture of balanced and thoughtful work. In doing so, we risk perpetuating the very hustle culture we claim to want to dismantle. This overemphasis on high-pressure performance isn't just confined to the hiring process—it extends into the realm of personal development as well. In our quest for self-improvement, we often chase the next "flavor of the month" trend, whether it's mastering the latest productivity hack, adopting a new mindset technique, or achieving work-life balance in yet another fashionable way. While these trends promise quick fixes, they can lead to a cycle of constant self-optimization that mirrors hustle culture, leaving little room for true rest and reflection. This relentless pursuit of the next breakthrough can make personal development feel more like a race than a meaningful journey.

The Personal Development Flavor of the Month

During my time at this organization, I gained extensive knowledge in various personality and team development frameworks, including Myers-Briggs Type Indicator, the DiSC Assessment, the Six Thinking Hats test, the True Colors test, the Five Dysfunctions of a Team, the Emotional Intelligence Test, Strengths-Finder, the 4 Personality Styles, and the Enneagram. You name it, we learned about it.

But there was never really any follow-up or usage beyond the training or a team professional development day. I wouldn't realize the lost ROI (return on investment) and gap in the market until much later when I developed my own training program, including a capacity management assessment where outcomes were mapped to tools and resources that people could easily learn without going back to a binder and rifling through pages and content trying to find what exactly they needed.

After my departure from corporate and as I took on my own clients and trained in Myers-Briggs, I would see people so amazed and finding value in learning more about who they were, and their tendencies and approaches to certain situations. I was hired by Big Corporate, school administrators, police services, mining companies, big banks, not-for-profits, and tech companies. Good facilitation is hard to come by, and I believe it's one of my areas of genius. I love holding the energy of a group and meeting them where they are while facilitating valuable sessions. The problem was: what were they expected to do afterwards? What tools did they have access to? How were they supposed to maintain the learning? What was the ROI of these soft skills?

I am personally a fan of the MBTI 16 personalities assessment. Derived from the original Myers-Briggs Type Indicator (MBTI) personality types, it allows you to better understand why you may show up the way you do at work and at home. It's not a tell-all or an exact science, but you take what you need from this tool to become more self-aware. After many years of using it, I became very curious as to which types might be more susceptible to burnout due to specific traits and tendencies. While individual experiences may vary, the following personality types are the top five generally considered more prone to burnout:

1, INFJ (Introverted, Intuitive, Feeling, Judging)—The Advocate

Why: INFJs often take on the emotional burdens of others and have a deep desire to help and support people. Their tendency to put others' needs before their own can lead to emotional exhaustion. They may also feel overwhelmed by the need to live up to their own ambitious standards and ideals.

2. ENFJ (Extraverted, Intuitive, Feeling, Judging)—The Protagonist

Why: ENFJs are driven to help others and can become overcommitted in their efforts to meet everyone's needs. Their powerful sense of responsibility and desire for harmony can lead to stress and burnout, especially when they neglect their own self-care.

3.INTJ (Introverted, Intuitive, Thinking, Judging)—The Architect

Why: INTJs are highly driven and perfectionistic. Their desire for efficiency and competence can lead them to overwork and take on too many responsibilities. They may also struggle with stress when things don't go according to plan.

4. INFP (Introverted, Intuitive, Feeling, Perceiving)—The Mediator
Why: INFPs are idealistic and sensitive. They can become disillusioned when reality doesn't match their ideals, leading to emotional exhaustion. Their tendency to internalize stress and avoid confrontation can also contribute to burnout.

5. ENTJ (Extraverted, Intuitive, Thinking, Judging)—The Commander
Why: ENTJs are goal-oriented and often take on leadership roles. Their drive for success and control can lead them to overextend themselves. They may neglect self-care and overlook the emotional needs of others, focusing heavily on achieving their objectives, which can result in burnout if they don't manage their energy and commitments effectively.

In my coaching practice, it's important to help people in their approach to personal and professional situations with a heightened awareness of their tendencies and ultimately how to reframe them to protect their capacity. Here are some common examples of factors contributing to burnout:

High Empathy
- Current Behavior: Types with strong Feeling (F) preferences are often more empathetic and may absorb others' emotions, leading to emotional exhaustion.

- **Reframe:** Instead of absorbing others' emotions, recognize and validate them without internalizing. Practice setting emotional boundaries by visualizing a protective barrier around your energy. Remind yourself that supporting others doesn't mean taking on their burdens.

Perfectionism
- **Current Behavior:** Types with Judging (J) preferences may set exacting standards for themselves and others, leading to stress when those standards are not met.

- **Reframe:** Shift your focus from perfection to progress. Celebrate small victories and recognize that imperfection is a natural part of growth. Remind yourself that achieving eighty percent of your goal is often more than enough and that done is better than perfect.

Overcommitment

- **Current Behavior:** Both Extraverted (E) and Introverted (I) types can overcommit in diverse ways—extraverts by taking on too many social or leadership roles, and introverts by taking on too much responsibility quietly.

- **Reframe:** Prioritize commitments by assessing their alignment with your core values and goals. Practice saying no by recognizing that each no allows you to say yes to what truly matters. For extraverts, focus on quality over quantity in your social and leadership roles. For introverts, delegate and share responsibilities to prevent quiet overburdening.

Idealism

- **Current Behavior:** Types with Intuitive (N) preferences often have strong ideals and can become disillusioned when reality doesn't meet their expectations.

- **Reframe:** Balance your ideals with a grounded sense of realism. Recognize the value in incremental progress and small wins. Practice gratitude for what is working well, even if it doesn't fully meet your ideal vision. Use your idealism as a guiding star but accept that the journey involves many imperfect steps.

By adopting these reframes, you can manage your burnout tendencies more effectively, honoring both your unique strengths and your capacity to thrive. Understanding these tendencies can help individuals recognize signs of burnout early and take steps to manage stress and maintain their well-being.

An elevated risk of burnout often derives from a combination of strong interpersonal or achievement-oriented skills paired with weak stress management or self-awareness abilities. Recognizing these patterns can help individuals take steps to balance their emotional intelligence skills, improve stress management techniques, and seek support when needed. Understanding these commonalities can help in identifying and addressing burnout risks by fostering better stress management, emotional awareness, and balance between personal and professional commitments.

My Own Big F Factor

When I reflect on the MBTI personality types, it's clear that those with the Feeling letter in their type are often the ones who take care of others, help, and are the first to volunteer on committees, ensuring team harmony. However, they are also the first ones to burn out. I now see a different side of why no one wanted to be the amiable ones. Despite the challenges, I wouldn't change this part of my personality, as it has led me to where I am today. The only thing I wish I had been taught is how to honor my giving nature while managing my capacity. Learning to balance my inclination to support others with the need to take care of myself would have made all the difference. It's a lesson I'm still learning, but it's crucial for sustaining both my well-being and my ability to contribute meaningfully.

Personally, this work wouldn't have been possible without some serious introspection. My deepest desires and tendencies came from very deep places in my life. Whether I'm attuned to it or not, trauma, grief, and big life events can fuel my personality into hyperdrive. My personal relationship with grief was one of these unconscious drivers that I finally was able to access decades after the initial trauma.

Chapter Five

Carrying Grief: How Loss Shapes Our Capacity

It's ok to cry, honey. You have to let it out, or it will just stay stuck inside and that's no good. — Pauline Sodtka (aka Grandma)

Diary Entry

*C*alled the doctor, reluctantly and with a lot of shame. (My doctor is a little younger than me and I know that if we had met outside of her practice, we would be good friends.)

I've been seeing my therapist for a while and we agreed it was time to share my depleted sense of self with her too.

So when I show up burned out, I feel like I am a failure and a fraudulent successful woman who doesn't know how to take care of herself.

Why call the doctor? Why now?

Yesterday I felt somewhat normal. Delusional and hopeful that I was cured.

Hey, maybe it was a temporary breakdown, and it will just go away on its own.

But somehow, my logic tells me that's simply not true.

I realized that my world was simple yesterday. No stress or worry for a couple of hours, which meant I could cope. No outside disturbances or infiltrations were able to disrupt the peace in my home.

This must be a part of the mental health mind games.

To be so lucid and know what the hell is happening in your brain but to also know you will relinquish all control because you simply have no mental capacity at the moment.

The desire to be happy is there. I want to laugh, to tell stories, but something has muted that function. It's just not possible to turn up the volume. So, I stay quiet, knowing my mind is controlled by my reptilian brain and has shut down certain functions to keep me safe and away from harm.

Healing must commence so that I can regain my voice.

Pandemic-induced Grief

The last few months of 2021, as the COVID pandemic wore on, were pivotal, painful, and particularly poignant. (I love good alliterations.)

We were exiting a pandemic, which had felt like a never-ending tunnel of unexpected twists and turns. While we all tried to roll with every jump scare around the corner, there was only so much we could endure before we became exhausted. And while that exhaustion set in and slowed us down, it also gave room for old trauma to rear its ugly head and sneak up on us. Repeatedly.

Unresolved parts of our past that we believed were long buried began to reappear again. Our subconscious, the gatekeeper of the trauma, lost track and the unearthing began, eroded by the pandemic fatigue. And suddenly, our collective trauma was showing. Our determined efforts to press forward felt futile. We lacked the emotional capacity to handle more setbacks or health scares. We were locked in a struggle against defeatism, and we needed to decide our next move—quickly.

I am not here to relive the traumas of the past, but to simply acknowledge that for many of us, they showed up during this already challenging and isolating time. I want to help you recognize that you made it. And maybe you're still working through it, like I am. But you're here. And you keep making decisions every day, for better or worse.

Grief is sneaky.

Grief lingers.

Grief isn't just due to the loss of a person.

It's the loss of many parts of lives.

It's a financial loss.

It's a loss of fertility.

It's a lost relationship.

It's a lost sense of self.

It's the loss of your career. Perhaps your identity.

It's the seemingly hopeless loss of freedom.

Many of us go through more than one of the above during our lifetime. And many of us don't or won't acknowledge the grief. And so it becomes part of our fabric, showing up when we least expect it, unannounced, uninvited, and intrusive, like a long-lost relative showing up at your door expecting to stay for a couple of weeks (or longer if you let them!).

Now what? Do we let it take over our thoughts? Our actions? Our behaviors? Our outlooks? Our destiny? The answer is, it will if we let it. But the other answer is, it won't if we choose not to let it.

I am not an expert on grief. But I am certainly connected to mine. In fact, much of who I am today is carved in grief. Through curiosity, exploration, therapy, and courageous conversations, I have learned to live with my grief and embrace it. Embrace grief? It may seem counterintuitive, but the more I dig in and face it, the more it becomes an important threading throughout the fabrics of my life.

My Personal Grief Story

I became a bereaved sister at the tender age of six years old.

My baby brother Gregory came into this world with an unexpected congenital illness called trisomy 13.

The odds were against him in even making it to full term.

And while he took a few breaths, he left us only hours after birth.

A trauma that would haunt us for decades.

This was so rare.

Forty years ago, grief was not talked about like it is today.

There were no internet articles or AI to look up to find out what to say (or not to say) to a grieving parent or sibling.

Therapy wasn't as available.

Grief wasn't something you brought up with friends. (That would make everyone uncomfortable.)

And shouldn't we be "over it" by now?

It wasn't until the last four years that I really began to explore my buried grief, always with me, a bag of rocks on my back. It impacted relationships, my outlook on life. It was heavy.

I carried it around like my armor. To protect me from any further loss.

Fear of loss became my way of being. My unconscious way of living in the world.

After a few years of therapy, I learned that fear of loss was the pattern and basis in every interaction of my life. I rarely went all in with important relationships and commitments. I would hold back to protect myself. I was scared I would lose and repeat the deep sense of loss just as I did when I was six. I was wired this way, and it wasn't my fault. Trauma will make you forget and will rewire the brain in the strangest ways. I know this now because I'm untangling the wiring that led me here. Trauma is a master of disguise.

The experience of losing a sibling is a trauma that permeates to the cellular level. It becomes embedded deep within, festering over time and resurfacing in unexpected ways, often triggered by moments even decades later. The grief, the replays, the questions, the rationalization, the self-pity, the anger and resentment, the unanswered questions—they were all too much to speak about. The most common question: *Why did this happen to us?*

And so, I detached myself from the event. I didn't realize I was doing this; it just became a coping mechanism. Emotional detachment enabled me to give what I could to those around me, to help make them smile because they had just experienced a loss so painful, that as a young child myself, I couldn't begin to understand. The healing process never really started until my mid-thirties when I began a business in speaking, facilitating, and coaching. I had to have the breakdown to experience the breakthrough.

Recently, I've been working on reconciling the abandoned grief that never went away. And one powerful question began to supercharge my healing: What did Gregory's passing do *for* me? This question had taken years to utter because I was convinced it sounded selfish, greedy, opportunistic. Misaligned with my definition of *grief*.

But the question opened a new space for me to explore that grief. It gave me back a part of my identity that I had muted so long ago. Grief has been a defining force in my life, shaping who I am and becoming the foundation of my story.

And everything started to make more sense. I created a business to help people release misaligned energy and to create capacity in their lives for experiences and people that really matter.If I can't help people make an impact, contribute to someone's well-being, or be seen for these identity-defining traits, then I am lost. And so is my identity.

It has taken me decades to discover how I identify in this world, and I am grateful every day for my baby brother. He may not have been strong enough to stick around with us physically on this crazy planet, but he has stuck around in a spiritual way to shape who I am today.

A Grief-centered Capacity Management Workshop

Serendipitously, along this grief journey, award winning singer-songwriter and actress Jully Black approached me to run a five-week course on grief for her community, called 100 Strong and Sexy. My senses tingled, and my heart stopped. Who was I to do this, but who was I not to do this? Having collaborated with her and another powerful woman, Nkechi Nwafor-Robinson, over the last few years, I gladly accepted and created a curriculum that served over fifty women who showed up for two hours each week for five weeks.

We learned how to process our grief. We learned how to replace language associated with grief that was no longer serving us. We learned how to live with grief and not bury it. We learned how to talk about it and articulate feelings where we didn't typically have the space to express and release the anguish.

This five-week experience is one I will never, ever forget. The tenderness, the sisterhood, the container of trust, the beautiful energy and supportive environment—they were all without judgment and with all the freedoms to release our deepest grief. I was inspired to share stories and normalize grief so that we can live with it peacefully, instead of kicking it around and tripping over it. It's my lived experience that I can *acknowledge* it.

When I introduced Dr. Lois Tonkin's 1996 article in my course, many attendees found themselves deeply moved by the concept she shared. In the article, Dr. Tonkin recounts a workshop where a mother who had lost her child years before created a powerful visual representation of her grief.

Look at Figure 5.1 below. At first, the mother drew an image of her life (her figures 1 and 2), shading it completely to represent how her grief initially consumed every aspect of her existence. She then sketched a second figure, showing what she had expected to happen over time: that her life would stay the same size, but her grief would gradually shrink and occupy less space. However, this wasn't what she experienced.

Instead, she drew a third figure (her Figure 3) that better reflected her reality. In this figure, the grief remained just as large as it was in the beginning, but her life around it had grown larger. The grief and loss never actually felt smaller, but her life slowly expanded around it. This allowed her to experience life beyond her grief, even though it was always present and still as significant.

This idea of "Growth Around Grief" resonated deeply with my course participants, offering them a new perspective on their own grief journeys. The concept provided comfort and hope, showing them that while grief may remain constant, their lives have the potential to grow and encompass new experiences, joy, and healing. Dr. Tonkin's example became a key point of discussion, helping attendees understand that it's possible to live fully, even in the presence of enduring grief.

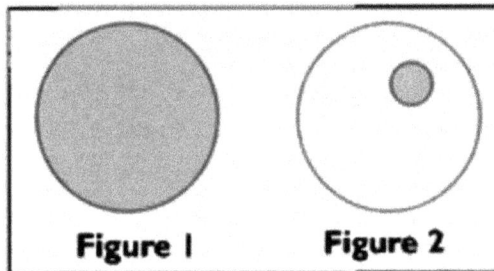

Figure 1   **Figure 2**

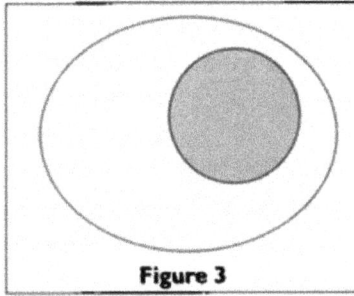

A diagram of a figure

Description automatically generated

Figure 5.1. The Growth of Life around Grief

Accessorizing Grief: A Concept That Offers Unexpected Comfort

When I came across an Instagram post by writer and illustrator Mari Andrew (that post is no longer available on the IG account), it struck a deep chord with me. The post featured a hand-drawn image of three bags in decreasing sizes—a large burlap sack, a briefcase, and a small purse—each labeled with the word "GRIEF." In her caption, Andrew shared her personal experience with grief, saying, "My dad died two years ago today. It's different for everyone, but my personal experience is that grief doesn't ever go away, but it does change shape, and it becomes something you can hold rather than something that overwhelms you—a part of you, rather than a burden."

Reading her words, I felt a wave of relief and understanding wash over me. She had perfectly captured what my family and I had been living with for over forty years since the loss of my brother. I was only six years old when he passed away, and those were some of my earliest memories. I didn't understand grief then, but I knew I didn't like the confusing and sad feelings that followed me.

As I grew older, grief became a constant, though unprocessed, presence in my life. It felt like carrying a forty-pound sack on my shoulders, a heavy burden that I didn't know how to articulate or share. Therapy helped me confront this weight, and I cried for the little girl who had to carry such an inexplicable heartache. Over time, that sack began to lighten, eventually becoming more of a heavy carry-on—still present, but not as overwhelming. Sometimes, I could even forget it was there.

Today, my grief has shifted again, resembling the small purse in Andrew's illustration. It's become more manageable and less burdensome, a part of me rather than something that overpowers me. Most days, it's light enough that I hardly notice it, like an accessory. Though there are still moments when it feels heavier, as if someone has slipped a brick inside.

What I've learned is that grief will likely never fully disappear, but I've grown strong enough to carry it. There will always be days when it hits me hard, wringing out my heart anew, but I find comfort in knowing that I can live with my grief. I know my brother would be proud of the resilience I've built in the face of this loss.

Mari Andrew's post might not resonate with everyone the way it did with me, but I'm grateful for her willingness to share her experience. It helped me make sense of something I'd been grappling with for a long time, and it reminded me that I'm not alone in this journey. Grief doesn't discriminate; it touches people from all walks of life, at any age. The more we talk about it, the better we can understand ourselves and find ways to move forward. That's what has helped me, and I hope it can help others too.

Figure 5.2. Illustration from Instagram post by Mari Andrew

How Unprocessed Grief Fuels Burnout

Grief is a profound emotional experience, one that can alter the course of your day, your relationships, and your very sense of self. When left unprocessed, grief does not remain a quiet companion; it lingers in the shadows, quietly sapping your strength. It shapes how you show up for your life, often leading to burnout without you even realizing the connection. Here's how:

The Weight of Emotional Overload

Grief brings with it a heavy burden of emotions: sadness, anger, guilt, confusion—all vying for your attention. When these emotions aren't acknowledged or processed, they accumulate and weigh you down. This emotional exhaustion becomes a silent thief of energy, slowly leading you toward burnout, where every task feels heavier than the last.

Diminished Coping Ability

When you're grieving, even the smallest stressor can feel insurmountable. Your capacity to cope is weakened; you're trying to hold back a dam that's already cracking. Unprocessed grief intensifies this fragility. Work deadlines, family obligations, and life's demands pile on, making burnout inevitable. The dam breaks.

Physical Manifestations of Grief

Grief doesn't live just in your heart and mind—it inhabits your entire body. Fatigue, headaches, a dull ache in your chest. These physical manifestations of grief deplete your energy reserves. You wake up already tired, face the day on empty, and by nightfall burnout tightens its grip.

Cognitive Overload: A Mind Stretched Thin

Grief clouds the mind. Your focus fades, memory slips, and making decisions feels like wading through fog. With your mind constantly preoccupied by sorrow, tasks that once seemed simple now require significant effort. This mental strain adds to the burnout, creating a cycle of decreased performance and mounting stress that feels impossible to escape.

Withdrawal and Isolation: Grief's Silent Wall

Grief often leads to isolation. You pull back from your connections, maybe without even noticing. The people who once provided support seem distant, and loneliness takes root. Without social connection, your resilience weakens, and burnout thrives in this emotional isolation. You end up feeling like you are carrying the weight of both grief and burnout alone.

Loss of Meaning and Purpose

When grief strikes, it often forces you to question what really matters. The sense of purpose that once guided your work and personal life begins to fade, replaced by a numbness that leaves you disconnected from your passions. This loss of meaning accelerates burnout, as the joy and fulfillment you once found in your efforts seem to disappear in the wake of sorrow. Grief and burnout are intimately linked. One feeds the other, and before you know it, you're trapped in an exhausting loop. Understanding this connection is vital—not just to acknowledge the grief you carry, but to prevent it from quietly eroding your sense of balance.

But you are not alone in this experience, and there is hope. Processing grief through therapy, support, or intentional self-care can be the key to breaking the burnout cycle. By recognizing the weight unprocessed grief places on your emotional and mental capacity, you open the door to healing—and in doing so, you honor both your grief and your own capacity to rebuild.

The Weight of Unprocessed Grief: A Story of Lost Capacity

In her book *How to Do the Work*, Dr. Nicole LePera explores the profound impact that unprocessed emotional trauma, particularly grief, can have on our overall well-being and capacity to function. She shares a personal experience of grief following the loss of her grandmother. She describes how her family, like many others, avoided emotional expression, which left her struggling to fully process the emotions of loss. Reflecting on this, she writes:

"I didn't know how to grieve, and neither did anyone around me. Instead, we pushed the emotions down, choosing to 'be strong,' which only distanced us further from ourselves and from each other. It wasn't until much later that I realized how important it was to allow myself to fully feel those emotions, to give space for grief, rather than bypassing it."

LePera emphasizes that unprocessed grief can manifest as emotional suppression, chronic stress, and even physical symptoms. Her story highlights the necessity of acknowledging and feeling our grief to heal fully. Inspired by her insights, I reflected on my own experiences and those of the people around me. Grief has been a constant thread in my life, shaping how I see the world and connect with others. As I moved through my own healing process, I came to realize that grief isn't something we can carry alone. We need a community—a space where people can hold one another through loss with understanding, compassion, and support. This realization became the driving force behind the Good Grief Gala.

I wanted to create a place where others could find the same support I longed for—a community that rallies together in times of loss. The Good Grief Gala was born from a desire to bring people together, to share our stories, and to remind each other that we don't have to navigate grief alone. Grief takes many forms, whether it's the loss of a loved one, a relationship, a job, or even a sense of self. It's about more than just acknowledging our grief—it's about reframing it as something that connects us, rather than isolates us.

This event isn't just about raising funds or awareness; it's about creating a shared, immersive experience where we can explore the depths of grief and discover ways to integrate it into our lives. I wanted it to reflect the support and love I've received on my journey, and I hope it can offer the same to others. More than anything, I want to show my children the power of community, the importance of helping one another, and the beauty of healing together.

Your Personal Grief: An Exercise

This exercise is meant to help you make a personal connection to what you've just read, as well as to gain clarity on how unprocessed grief may be impacting your life.

1. **Find a quiet space** where you won't be interrupted for the next few minutes. Grab a journal or something to write with, or simply reflect in your mind if writing isn't your preference.

2. **Take a deep breath** and allow yourself to think about your own experiences of grief, whether recent or from years ago. Consider the emotions and memories that surface, without judgment.

3. **Answer the following questions honestly and compassionately.** The goal is to explore, not to criticize yourself. Let these questions guide your thoughts:

   - Have you noticed any physical or emotional changes in yourself that could be linked to grief?

   - In what ways has grief affected your ability to cope with stress or daily tasks?

   - Do you find yourself withdrawing from others or feeling detached from work or personal relationships?

   - How has grief affected your sense of purpose or accomplishment in your career or personal life?

4. **As you reflect, notice any patterns** that emerge. Are there certain areas where grief seems to impact you more strongly? What do you recognize about the way grief and burnout might be connected in your life?

5. **Give yourself permission** to feel whatever comes up. Whether it's sadness, frustration, or even relief, all your emotions are valid. The purpose of this reflection is to honor your own experience with grief and burnout.

6. **Take a moment to process.** Once you've gone through these questions, take another deep breath. If you're journaling, you might want to jot down any additional thoughts that came up. If you're reflecting mentally, give yourself a few quiet moments to sit with what you've uncovered.

Remember, this exercise is for your growth and understanding. By reflecting on these questions, you're creating space to recognize and process the grief that may be silently fueling burnout in your life. This awareness is the first step toward healing and regaining balance.

This page is intentionally left blank for you to capture some notes, thoughts, and reflections on what we've covered in Part 1: Audit Your Capacity.

PART 2: OPTIMIZE YOUR CAPACITY

Chapter Six

Am I the CEO of My Capacity?

What you resist not only persists but will grow in size. — Carl Jung

Diary Entry

*T*oday, I asked myself a tough question: Am I really the CEO of my own capacity? If so, am I making the right decisions?

Looking at my own CHIEFF framework — Career, Health, Intellectual, Emotional, Financial, Fun — I see cracks forming. My Career dominates, leaving me overcommitted. Health? Neglected. Exercise and rest always seem to take a backseat when work calls. Intellectually, I'm stretched thin, consuming more than I can process. My Emotional capacity feels drained, as I'm always supporting others, yet rarely giving myself grace.

Even financially, the pressure to say yes for more income looms, despite knowing it could drain me further. And Fun? It's been sidelined, a forgotten part of the balance I once valued.

I realize I've lost touch with my own capacity. I need to pause, reflect, and make better choices — starting now.

I resign from overcommitment.

I honor my capacity.

Tomorrow, I will *choose* what truly matters.

CHIEFF of Your Capacity: Surrendering to the Process

I'll never forget one keynote where I introduced the CHIEFF™ of Your Capacity tool. My keynotes are always interactive because the goal is to leave participants with a new perspective, an experience, or a resource they can immediately apply or take home. It's always top of mind when creating keynotes for my clients.

This particular group was composed of men in the construction industry. You can imagine their professional development rarely involves evaluating their intellectual achievement or emotional state. Asking them to do this exercise might have been a bit of a stretch, but I was all in. I remember the eye rolls and crossed arms, signaling, *What is this woman going to teach us?* Still, I was determined because I knew the power of this exercise.

I handed out laminated worksheets and dry-erase markers, so they could take them home and redo the exercise anytime. One man raised his hand and said, "I don't need to do this. I already know my capacity. I'm fine. I do well with my family and my career. I don't need this." I told him that was fine and encouraged him to participate just for fun.

As I explained the tool and walked them through the steps, I challenged them to think about the various parts of their lives and evaluate the quality of their capacity, not just the time spent. Slowly, I saw shoulders drop, eyes fix on their worksheets, and a few smiles appear. A calm, almost transformational sense of satisfaction rippled through the room, and I knew I was onto something.

Most of the men completed the exercise, and at the end I thanked everyone. As I wrapped up, four men lined up to speak to me. The first in line was the man who had insisted he didn't need to participate. With tears in his eyes, he said, "Thank you so much for this hour. I've realized I don't spend enough quality time at home. I give everything to work but not enough to my kids and family. And as you can see," he said, patting his belly, "I haven't taken care of my health, which scares me. So, thank you."

These moments are incredibly powerful. In just fifteen minutes, when people take the time to evaluate the quality of their capacity, they shine a light on areas needing improvement. Once illuminated, there's no denying or hiding from them. The only thing left to do is give those areas the attention and energy they deserve. It's a simple yet profound step toward bettering ourselves.

The Attention Economy Has a Bigger Impact Than You Might Think

Attention is our most precious commodity, and it's constantly under siege. Numerous books, such as *The Attention Economy* and *The Attention Merchants*, explore how companies, traditional media, and social platforms compete fiercely for our focus to boost brand visibility, loyalty, and profitability. Unfortunately, this relentless battle for our attention often comes at a significant cost to us, draining our mental resources and leaving us more susceptible to decision fatigue.

Decision fatigue is the wear and tear on our ability to make good choices as the day goes on. The more decisions we face, the more our mental energy depletes, leading to poorer decisions when we're tired. This highlights the importance of conserving our brainpower for the big stuff and tackling critical decisions when our cognitive capacity is at its peak.

Our capacity to make decisions is closely tied to the number of choices we navigate daily, a topic of ongoing research. Studies suggest that our unconscious brain makes decisions about seven seconds before our conscious mind catches up. In one study, participants were asked to press a yes or no button and identify when they decided which to press. Using MRI scans, researchers could accurately predict the participants' choices up to seven seconds before they consciously made them. This finding raises fascinating questions about the unconscious information we rely on to make decisions and whether this process can be rewired.

Understanding these insights into our decision-making processes emphasizes the importance of forming commitment habits and patterns that streamline our choices. By minimizing unnecessary decisions, we can preserve our cognitive resources for more significant and impactful choices.

The Paradox of Choice

In a world where the freedom to choose is often equated with the pinnacle of personal empowerment and happiness, Barry Schwartz stands out as a voice of reason and clarity. One of the thought-provoking challenges introduced by Schwartz, a renowned psychologist and professor who has dedicated his career to unraveling one of the most pervasive myths of our time, is that more choice bring more happiness. The notion, deeply embedded in modern consumer culture, is that having more options empowers individuals, enabling them to tailor their lives to their exact preferences and desires. However, his research reveals a startling paradox: instead of liberating us, an overabundance of choices can lead to anxiety, indecision, and even dissatisfaction.

Drawing from his influential book, *The Paradox of Choice: Why More Is Less*, Schwartz provides a comprehensive exploration of how the sheer volume of choices we face—whether in shopping, career decisions, or personal relationships—can overwhelm us. This phenomenon, known as "choice overload," can make it increasingly difficult to make decisions, ultimately undermining our happiness.

He introduces us to the psychological mechanisms behind this paradox, illustrating how the pressure to make the perfect choice can lead to paralysis and regret. He contrasts the experiences of "maximizers," who strive to make the best possible decision, with "satisficers," who settle for good enough, highlighting how these different approaches to decision-making impact our mental health and sense of fulfillment. Through compelling real-world examples and rigorous scientific analysis, he invites us to reconsider our assumptions about choice. He argues that, in many cases, less truly is more, advocating for a more mindful approach to decision-making that can lead to greater contentment and well-being.

In this chapter, we're diving into a new way of thinking about choice and happiness. We'll explore how having more options doesn't always lead to a happier life, and we'll challenge ourselves to rethink how we deal with the constant barrage of decisions in today's world. Get ready to see things differently as we unpack the paradox of choice and what it really means for finding satisfaction in our lives.

A Real-World Example

Imagine this: you're at the grocery store, armed with a shopping list and the responsibility of hosting a big family feast. You confidently stride down the aisles, ticking off items with ease—until you hit the salad dressing section. Suddenly, you're confronted with a bewildering array of over eighty salad dressing options, each one screaming for your attention with vibrant labels and bold claims. As you stand there, you can almost hear Barry Schwartz's voice echoing in your head from his TED talk on the paradox of choice. You're starting to feel his conclusion deeply and in real time! What *should* be a simple decision becomes a complex labyrinth of considerations.

You remember Aunt Bertha's celiac disease, so gluten-free is a must. Then there's Samantha, who's allergic to nuts. Your mother is on a diet, demanding a low-fat option. And, of course, cousin Tim has recently become vegan. Each thought adds a layer of pressure, and the once simple task of picking a salad dressing becomes an epic quest. Your mind races as you pick up and put down bottles, scrutinizing ingredients, and nutritional information. The aisle seems to stretch longer, and your confidence wavers. Finally, with a mix of desperation and resignation, you grab one that seems to tick most of the boxes.

As you approach the checkout, a wave of doubt washes over you. Did you choose the right one? What if Aunt Bertha can't eat it? What if Samantha has an allergic reaction? What if your mom gives you the disappointed look because it's not low-fat enough? At the register, the cashier notices your frazzled state and asks, "Honey, are you ok?" You muster a weak smile and nod, but inside you're second-guessing every choice. As you leave the store, you're already anticipating regret, convinced that your selection will ruin the whole feast. This comical yet painfully real scenario highlights the decision fatigue many of us face. Whether it's choosing a salad dressing or making more significant life decisions, the abundance of options can paralyze us. Decision-making filters—like people-pleasing, FOMO, comparison, and perfectionism—further cloud our judgment and drain our capacity. The paradox of choice teaches us that more isn't always better. When faced with a plethora of options, especially for meaningful decisions like money management, health, or family matters, the overwhelm can be crippling. Recognizing this, we can strive to simplify our choices and focus on what truly matters, reducing the mental load and preserving our capacity.

But the challenge doesn't end there. The overwhelming number of choices can lead to a deeper issue: self-sabotage. When we're unable to navigate the sea of options effectively, we often engage in behaviors that undermine our goals and well-being. This self-destructive pattern, driven by fear, doubt, or a need for control, can prevent us from achieving the balance and fulfillment we seek. Understanding the roots and manifestations of self-sabotage is crucial in our journey toward making more meaningful and manageable choices.

From Overwhelm to Insight: Navigating Choices and Overcoming Self-Sabotage

I've been reflecting a lot lately, especially about my self-worth—what I value, what I associate with my identity, and how these things influence my behavior. When I feel undervalued or unappreciated at work, I revert to a long-standing habit that's been with me for twenty-five years: retail therapy. It's a recurring cycle. When work feels burdensome or I feel worthless, I seek solace in this habit for a temporary boost. It's all about the dopamine hits that make me feel good. I've essentially trained myself to do this over the years. I'm working on this reaction with my therapist, who has mentioned lacking concrete goals, being too spontaneous, and having zero discipline—all ingredients for overspending.

At the end of the day, it all comes down to self-worth—what I value and how I tie my worth to it. When your self-worth takes a hit, you try to fix it with whatever makes you feel good again, even if it's just temporary happiness. But it's counterproductive: you end up feeling worse, and then shame kicks in and you beat yourself up over the whole thing. You think, *Man, I could've done better.* But unless you really work on that self-worth stuff, those patterns will just keep repeating.

And it's not just about me; it affects my family and friends too. Nobody wants to feel desperate or like they're barely keeping their head above water. That's when bad choices happen, and that's when burnout sets in. You're just scrambling to find something to make you feel better, to patch up whatever went wrong. But real change comes from doing the hard work by focusing on self-worth. That's the real deal right there.

Imagine your capacity as a bucket filled with water, representing your energy and wellness. However, this bucket often has cracks and leaks caused by the most common offenders: comparisonitis, multitasking, people-pleasing, FOMO, and perfectionism. Each of these factors steadily drains your capacity, leaving the bucket nearly empty and you feeling depleted and overwhelmed. When we define wellness, it's crucial to recognize that each person's bucket and its leaks are unique. Wellness looks different to everyone, as we all have varying sources of leaks and different methods of replenishing our water. By identifying and addressing these leaks, we can better manage our capacity and maintain our overall wellness.

The Dopamine Fix and Spending

In his book *The Psychology of Money*, Morgan Housel delves into the behavioral aspects of personal finance, highlighting how psychological factors influence financial decisions. One of the key insights he provides is the role of dopamine in driving spending behaviors. Dopamine, a neurotransmitter associated with pleasure and reward, can significantly impact our financial choices, often leading to impulsive spending.

His key insights on dopamine and spending are:

1. **Reward System:** The brain's reward system, powered by dopamine, can lead to a cycle of seeking immediate gratification through spending. When people purchase something new, dopamine is released, creating a temporary feeling of happiness and excitement. This can become addictive, causing individuals to seek out new purchases to maintain that high.

2. **Impulse Buying:** The instant pleasure derived from dopamine can lead to impulse buying, where purchases are made without careful consideration of long-term consequences. This behavior is often driven by marketing tactics that trigger emotional responses, making it hard to resist the urge to spend.

3. **The Hedonic Treadmill:** The concept of the hedonic treadmill is that individuals quickly return to a baseline level of happiness after a positive or negative event, including purchases. The temporary boost in happiness from buying something new fades, leading to a continuous cycle of spending in pursuit of that fleeting dopamine rush.

4. **Financial Stress and Burnout:** The pursuit of dopamine through spending can lead to financial stress, as individuals may find themselves in debt or unable to save for future needs. This financial stress can contribute to burnout, as the pressure to maintain a certain lifestyle or manage debt can be overwhelming.

5. **Mindful Spending:** Individuals take a step back to consider the long-term value and impact of their purchases. By recognizing the influence of dopamine on their spending habits, individuals can make more intentional financial decisions that align with their values and long-term goals.

In today's fast-paced world, the rush of dopamine we get from spending, whether it's through retail therapy, online shopping sprees, or the allure of the latest gadgets, can create a temporary sense of fulfillment. This instant gratification, however, often leads to a cycle of perpetual consumption, leaving us feeling overwhelmed and out of control. It's easy to become trapped in a pattern where the pursuit of momentary pleasure overshadows our long-term goals and overall well-being.

Taking control of your capacity means stepping back, evaluating your options, and making deliberate choices about where to invest your resources. You need to recognize that true fulfillment comes not from the transient excitement of spending but from building a life that is sustainable and balanced. By doing so, you can create a more meaningful and purpose-driven existence, where your actions are aligned with your core values and long-term aspirations.

Evaluate Your Role as CHIEFF of Your Capacity

To begin, draw a horizontal line on a piece of paper and with a vertical line on each end. Within each of the CHIEFF categories, *allocate a percentage of time* you spend on each in an average week or month. Some people calculate this down to the hour, while others use rough estimates. Mapping these percentages on the line will give you a visual reflection of how you spend your time.

Next, evaluate the *quality of the capacity* you bring to each category. Reflect on three core components:

1. **Energy:** Are you bringing your best energy? Are you taking care of yourself to perform well?

2. **Purpose:** Are you connected to your purpose? Do you see the value you bring, and is it fulfilling?

3. **Connection:** Do you feel supported by your ecosystem, such as colleagues or family? Are you plugged into a network?

As you go through this exercise, ask yourself how you feel about the results. Some people might find it difficult to confront these realities, while others may see it as an opportunity for improvement or a reality check.

This exercise is powerful because it helps you dissect different areas of your life and look at the quality of your capacity in a structured way. It provides insights into where you can improve and how to optimize your capacity. By regularly reflecting on these aspects, you can make meaningful changes to enhance your overall well-being and effectiveness.

Balancing all the different areas of our lives—Career, Health, Intellectual growth, Emotional well-being, Financial security, and Fun—isn't always easy. At some point, though, even the most committed person needs to step back and rethink how they're playing the game. Just as an athlete might sit out a competitive event to recharge and avoid injury, we need to know when it's time to pull ourselves out of the constant hustle. Taking that intentional pause helps us realign with what really matters. In the next chapter, we'll dive into the "art of resignation"—learning how to step away from commitments that no longer fit, creating space for what truly aligns with our values and sets us on a more meaningful, sustainable path forward.

Chapter Seven

Resignation Without Regret: Reclaiming Ambition Without Burnout

Burnout should never be the price of ambition. — Melanie Sodka

Diary Entry

*M*y lawyer and I were talking today and he shared with me that it takes, on average, two months to recover from burnout. If this is true, and this is my third diagnosis of burnout, then I'm on my second attempt to recover from my first.

This hit me like a ton of bricks. Something has to give.

Currently, my calendar is packed from morning to night, and the weekends are no better. The guilt of letting anyone down keeps me up at night. I worry about the shame I'll feel if I have to back out of something. What will people think? Will they see me as weak? As a failure? The thought paralyzes me.

Why am I sacrificing my peace for all these commitments? It's hard to admit, but I am simply too tired to keep up.

Today, I had a moment of clarity amidst the chaos. While juggling yet another request for my time, I realized I have to resign from something. I don't know what yet, but I know it's necessary. The idea terrifies me. I'm scared of the disapproval, the disappointment from colleagues, friends, and even myself. It's a battle between my desire to succeed and my need for sanity.

I'm trying to be kind to myself, but it's hard. I feel like I'm failing because I can't match my ambition with the energy required.

I wish I had more answers, but for now, all I can do is take it one step at a time. Tomorrow I'll try to find the courage to have those difficult conversations, to set

boundaries, and to reclaim some of my peace. Maybe, just maybe, I'll learn that it's ok to say no and that doing less doesn't mean being less.

For tonight, I will try to find solace in the decision to start making changes. It's a small step, but it's a step towards a life where I can breathe again.

Making Space: Letting Go for Growth

Let's delve into resignation—not the kind involving quitting a job, but the kind where you let go of the things holding you back. We all encounter distractions in our lives, such as binge-watching Netflix, endless social media scrolling, or playing addictive games on our phones. These habits consume our time and energy. It's time to reassess and eliminate these distractions. Reprogramming our habits and rituals is essential for progress. You likely already recognize which habits are detrimental. Reflect for a moment: what is your most significant time-wasting habit? Identifying it is the first step toward change.

In Robin Sharma's *The Monk Who Sold His Ferrari*, he tells the story of two lawyers, one older and one younger, both successful in their careers. The older lawyer, however, faced burnout—poor diet, overwork, and failed relationships led to a heart attack. This crisis prompted him to seek wisdom from monks in the mountains. Upon returning, transformed into a monk himself, he shared his insights with the younger lawyer over tea. As he poured the tea, he continued until it overflowed. The younger lawyer, puzzled, asked why. The monk responded with a profound lesson: "Just like this cup, you seem to be full of your own ideas. And how can any more go in … until you first empty your cup?" This highlights the importance of making space for new growth by letting go of the old.

The key takeaway is the importance of creating space in our lives by letting go of distractions and obligations that drain our time and energy. This means learning to say no, even when it's uncomfortable. Many of us have been conditioned to say yes to almost everything—taking on extra tasks at work, attending social events we're too tired for, or volunteering our time when we're already overwhelmed. This reflexive *yes* often stems from a desire to be seen as dependable and capable.

Yet, deep down, we know we can't do it all. Every *yes* comes at the cost of something else—whether it's our rest, peace of mind, or time with loved ones. Despite this, we struggle to say no because it feels like we're letting others down or admitting we can't handle it all. This fear of disappointing others or stepping out of our comfort zones keeps us stuck in a cycle of stress and burnout.

But constantly saying yes without considering the impact on our well-being pulls us away from what truly matters. Learning to say no isn't about rejecting opportunities—it's about recognizing our limits, honoring our priorities, and giving ourselves the space to grow. It's about breaking free from the conditioning that tells us we must always say yes and embracing the strength that comes from setting healthy boundaries.

When managing our time, it's easy to feel like there's never enough to go around. We often convince ourselves that we're too busy to squeeze in everything we want or need to do. But there's one truth we can't ignore: how we choose to spend our time directly impacts our well-being. This brings me to a quote from Jim Rohn that resonates deeply every time I come across it: "Take care of your body. It's the only place you have to live." It's a powerful reminder that prioritizing our time wisely isn't just ticking off tasks on a to-do list—it's investing in our health and future. The solution lies in simplification. Emulate the approach of Steve Jobs or Mark Zuckerberg, for example: maintain a simple wardrobe and streamline your morning routine to expand your capacity.

Humans tend to over-complicate things due to a combination of cognitive biases, fear of failure, and societal pressures. Our brains naturally seek patterns and create elaborate scenarios to make sense of the world, often leading to unnecessary complexity. The fear of missing crucial details or making mistakes can drive us to add layers of analysis and precaution. Additionally, societal norms and expectations to appear competent and thorough can pressure individuals to overthink and over-complicate tasks. Ultimately, this tendency stems from a desire for control and a fear of uncertainty, making simple solutions seem inadequate or incomplete. Ultimately, you need to make space for what truly matters. Resign from activities and habits that hinder you and focus on those that invigorate you. It's not quitting; it's reclaiming your time and energy to live a fulfilling life.

Let's give it a shot! Here are two exercises I facilitate during my keynotes.

"I Resign from …"

First, review chapter 3 and then pick something to resign from or choose something that isn't serving you—a mindset, a habit, a current commitment or anything for that matter.

Second, select something from chapter 6 that you'd like to focus more on by reviewing your CHIEFF exercise.

Finally, complete this statement:

I resign from _____ (e.g., a mindset, habit, or commitment) **in order to create capacity for** _____ (e.g., more time with family, going for walks, or more social time).

How do you feel? What was that like? What if I encouraged you to call someone or to read that resignation statement to someone today? Would you do it? How could you add some accountability?

Jenga

Imagine playing Jenga, where the goal is to keep the tower from toppling over while players remove pieces of it. Each move requires strategy and care, ensuring that each block removed doesn't disrupt the tower's balance and even make it topple. Now, envision that this tower represents your day or week.

Every time someone asks for something and you say yes, or every time you commit to something new, you must remove a block. The average person says yes numerous times throughout the week, but do we really keep track of these commitments? We track everything else in our lives: calories, weight, bank accounts, temperature, time … but are we tracking our commitments and the capacity needed to fulfill them? When we start to consider our capacity in intellectual, emotional, and physical terms, things get complicated. Saying yes to a family member requires emotional capacity. Committing to a new work project demands intellectual capacity. Signing up for a 5k or marathon needs physical capacity. Many of us underestimate the capacity required for these commitments.

So, back to Jenga. Did you say yes while your tower was solid, or was it already wobbly? Often, we press our luck, thinking we can get away with it. We adopt an "I'll show them" mentality, but no one is asking us to prove our capacity limits. We place these demands on ourselves. In Jenga, there's a fear that each block you pull out might make the tower topple. This fear parallels what we feel about the parts of our lives we carefully balance. But unlike Jenga, I'm talking about removing the *non-essential* pieces of your life, about resigning from commitments that no longer serve you.

Imagine pulling out the pieces you don't want. What I hope you'll learn from this book is that you can remove entire floors, and your tower will still stand strong. This is the art of resignation—emotionally engineering your life by removing unnecessary commitments and still maintaining a solid, balanced structure.

Deconstructing Hustle Culture

Practicing the art of resignation myself, I began to realize there was so much hypocrisy in this hustle culture we've been swept into, so I engaged with individuals to ponder a simple question: what does *hustle* mean to you right now? It was a prompt to reflect on the most common words of advice or wisdom we encounter when it comes to hard work. I heard familiar phrases like "Sleep when you're dead," "Be the first to arrive, last to leave," and "No pain, no gain." These were the mantras I grew up with, guiding principles in the world of business.

However, a moment of realization hit me when I began hearing contradictory advice. Suggestions like proper sleep, regular meals, Pilates and yoga, meditation breaks, family time, and self-care routines contradicted everything I had previously learned about the grind of business. It made me pause and question the validity of what I thought I knew.

This introspection deepened when in 2023 I hosted a guest on my Hustle Hypocrisy™ podcast. She had left her corporate job due to a battle with breast cancer at just forty years old. Despite her success and accolades, she confessed to secretly hoping for more treatment to avoid returning to work—a troubling sign of burnout and deep dissatisfaction. Her story underscored a fundamental flaw in our work culture. The signs of her burnout were apparent long before her illness manifested. This led me to the realization that achieving work-life balance is not a one-time accomplishment but an ongoing negotiation. Life's unexpected challenges require us to constantly reassess and readjust our priorities.

Resilience emerged as a key concept in this discussion. It's often misunderstood as bouncing back quickly from adversity. In reality, it's the daily practices that prepare us for life's uncertainties, helping us maintain calm and control amidst chaos. Resignation as an artform. In a world of endless opportunities and commitments, knowing when to gracefully decline is vital for preserving our well-being—acknowledging our limits and making choices that prioritize our health and relationships over fleeting achievements. I invite you to embrace the art of resignation, to relinquish commitments that no longer serve you in favor of nurturing what truly matters. Let's engage in dialogue, share stories, and collectively redefine what it means to hustle with purpose and integrity.

Writing my first resignation letter was not easy. But today, that letter symbolizes the foundation of my business—Capacity Creator Corporation, where I help others prevent burnout and help capacity management. The transformation didn't happen overnight; it was a journey filled with countless bumps in the road. But now I understand. I see the allure of the hustle, the tempting rewards for sacrificing so much—the fame, the likes, the awards, the prestige. I was ambitious and driven. But through this painful journey, I learned an essential lesson: burnout doesn't have to be the price of ambition.

Declining Requests

Before you go onto the next chapter, read the following scenarios and potential responses to ease your resignation angst. Keep in mind ...

- It's not always just saying no but also *seeking clarification* in your response.

- Using some of these responses will start to *teach people how to approach you* with future requests.

- Using some of these common capacity management situations and responses in conjunction with the other capacity tools will *insulate and protect your bandwidth.*

- *Saying no is not easy*, but there are gracious, mutually understood, and respectful ways to decline.

Here are some real-life scenarios in which you might have to say no:

Social Invitations: Being invited to a social event or party that you don't feel like attending but you agree to because you don't want to disappoint the host or miss out on potential fun (FOMO).

Response: "Thank you so much for the invite, but I don't have the capacity for that right now. I hope you have a wonderful time!"

Work Commitments: Taking on additional tasks or projects at work, even when your schedule is already full, because you want to appear diligent and reliable or you fear letting the team down.

Response: "I appreciate the opportunity to help with this project, but I don't have the capacity for that at the moment. Perhaps we can revisit this in the future."

Family Obligations: Agreeing to family gatherings or activities you aren't interested in because of family expectations or fear of being seen as unsupportive or uncaring.

Response: "I wish I could join the family gathering, but I don't have the capacity for that right now. Please understand."

Volunteer Activities: Committing to volunteer for school, community events, or charity work despite feeling overwhelmed, because you want to be seen as helpful and generous.

Response: "I would love to help with the event, but I don't have the capacity for that currently. Maybe next time."

Financial Contributions: Donating money to causes or lending money to friends or family even when you can't really afford it, out of a sense of obligation or fear of damaging relationships.

Response: "I'm really sorry, but I don't have the capacity to contribute financially at the moment. I hope you understand."

Networking Events: Attending professional networking events or meetups, even when you're exhausted or uninterested, because you feel it's necessary for career advancement.

Response: "*Thank you for inviting me to the networking event, but I don't have the capacity for that right now. Let's connect another time.*"

Social Media Engagement: Participating in social media challenges, trends, or group activities to avoid feeling left out or peer pressure, even when you don't genuinely want to.

Response: "*I appreciate the tag, but I don't have the capacity for that challenge right now. Maybe another time.*"

Peer Requests: Saying yes to helping a friend or colleague move, assist with a project, or run errands, even when it's inconvenient, because you don't want to appear unkind or unhelpful.

Response: "*I wish I could help you with your project, but I don't have the capacity for that at the moment. I'm sure you'll do great!*"

Holiday Celebrations: Agreeing to host or participate in elaborate holiday celebrations and traditions that you find stressful or unenjoyable, just to avoid disappointing others.

Response: "*I love our holiday traditions, but I don't have the capacity for hosting this year. Let's keep it simple.*"

Parent-Teacher Associations (PTA): Volunteering for roles or tasks within parent-teacher associations or other school-related activities despite lacking time or interest, due to societal expectations or peer pressure from other parents.

Response: "*I'm grateful for the opportunity to volunteer, but I don't have the capacity for that role right now. Thank you for considering me.*"

In mastering the art of resignation, the crucial takeaway is that saying no does not make you a bad person. It's common to feel guilt and shame when declining commitments, as these emotions are often rooted in behaviors learned in childhood. Research indicates that the way we perceive and express refusal is heavily influenced by the family dynamics and cultural norms we grew up with. In some families, saying no might have been seen as rude or disappointing, instilling a fear of missing out (FOMO) and a compulsion to always agree.

Hustle culture capitalizes on these ingrained fears and behaviors, perpetuating a cycle of urgency and overcommitment. The mantra of "hurry up and commit before it's too late" exploits our reluctance to refuse, pressuring us to take on more than we can manage. By understanding and deconstructing these learned behaviors, we can begin to navigate our commitments more mindfully.

Resigning from obligations that no longer serve us is not only an act of self-care but also a step towards reclaiming our time and energy. It empowers us to say yes to what truly matters, fostering a more balanced and fulfilling life.

Chapter Eight

The Hustle Paradox: Striving for Balance in a Contradictory Culture

You'll miss 100% of the shots you don't take. — attributed to Wayne Gretzky

Diary Entry

*K*eep hustling, they say.

    Don't let them see you sweat.

But be vulnerable so they know you're real.

Fake it till you make it.

But join a community to share your struggles.

You can sleep when you're dead.

But make sure you get seven hours so you can perform well.

You must meet the customer where they are.

But you can't be everything to everyone, so pick a lane.

It's now or never.

But more opportunities will always come.

Keep hustling, they say.

Be responsive. Answer within sixty mins for better reviews.

But don't get distracted by replying to all of them, or you'll tank your productivity.

Don't make the same mistake eighty percent of people are making.

Do this and see your job prospects increase!

But don't be too pushy or you'll be ignored.

The Hypocrisy in the Hustle Culture

I embarked on a journey to study hustle culture because I was deeply concerned about how it was shaping our work environments and communities. The relentless drive for success, often glorified and pushed by mainstream media and social influencers, was creating an illusion that constant productivity equates to worthiness. I aimed to demystify this notion and uncover the paradox at its core. Through interviews with individuals from diverse backgrounds and ages across different countries, I began to see how this not-so-underground culture was infiltrating our lives. The cost of this infiltration is staggering, with healthcare expenses for stress-related illnesses and burnout skyrocketing. According to statistics from Deloitte, burnout affects seventy-seven percent of professionals, leading to increased absenteeism and decreased productivity, further straining our healthcare system and economy.

Interestingly, high-profile individuals like Gary Vaynerchuk, who once championed the hustle culture, are rethinking their opinions. Vaynerchuk has recently started promoting the importance of sleep and self-care, signaling a shift in the narrative. This change is critical, and in my personal experience, hustle culture impacts men and women differently, with women often facing higher levels of stress due to juggling professional and personal responsibilities. The pervasive pressure to hustle not only affects mental and physical health but also perpetuates gender disparities in the workplace. (Hutto, Orgad.)

Hustle culture has been shown to have a disproportionately negative impact on women, particularly women of color, due to a variety of social, economic, and cultural factors. Research highlights several ways in which hustle culture affects women more than men:

1. **Double Burden:** Women often bear the "second shift," which refers to the unpaid labor of childcare and household responsibilities on top of their paid work. The pressure to engage in side-hustles or work long hours exacerbates this burden, leaving women more susceptible to burnout and stress-related health issues, as during the COVID-19 pandemic.

2. **Economic Pressures:** Women, especially Black and Latina mothers,

are often the primary breadwinners in their families. These women face additional challenges in balancing work and family life, as they are more likely to struggle with affordable childcare and earn less than their white counterparts. This economic pressure forces many to engage in hustle culture out of necessity rather than choice, leading to further exploitation and reduced opportunities for advancement.

3. **Cultural Expectations:** The notion of the "girlboss" or "mompreneur" has been glamorized in media, pushing women to embrace entre-preneurial endeavors alongside traditional jobs. However, this often sets unrealistic expectations and perpetuates a toxic work culture that prioritizes productivity over well-being. For many women, especially those from marginalized backgrounds, the promise of success through sheer hard work is often unattainable due to systemic barriers.

To shed light on these issues and foster meaningful conversations, I began hosting the *Hustle Hypocrisy* podcast. It explores the realities of hustle culture across different industries, examining its impact on people's career experiences, work trajectories, and mental health. The podcast aims to demystify the meaning of hustle and explore how and why society glorifies the grind. The goal is to redefine the word *hustle* and inspire others to reduce the frenetic pace associated with it. By reconciling our relationship with hustle culture, the featured con-versations hosted on the podcast aim to increase mental well-being and evoke ways to establish a personal approach to what can be referred to as sustainable ambition. Through these discussions, I challenge the glorification of hustle culture and promote healthier, more sustainable ways of working.

To help set the stage, here are some powerful yet contradictory hustle quotes that have informed a generation to work harder, often at the expense of their health:

1. **Elon Musk:** "No one ever changed the world on 40 hours a week."

   ○ Emphasizes the need for extreme dedication and long hours to achieve world-changing success.

2. **Gary Vaynerchuk:** "You have to work your face off to get what you want."

- Underscores the belief that relentless effort and sacrifice are necessary to achieve success.

3. **Steve Jobs:** "I'm convinced that about half of what separates the successful entrepreneurs from the non-successful ones is pure perseverance."

    - Suggests that sheer determination and constant effort are key to success, potentially downplaying the importance of balance.

4. **Mark Cuban:** "Work like there is someone working 24 hours a day to take it all away from you."

    - Promotes the idea of working incessantly out of fear of losing one's achievements.

5. **Dwayne Johnson:** "Be humble. Be hungry. And always be the hardest worker in the room."

    - Encourages continuous effort and striving to outwork everyone else, which can lead to burnout.

6. **Grant Cardone:** "You sleep like you're rich, I'm up like I'm broke."

    - Implies that to achieve success, one must sacrifice rest and constantly hustle.

7. **Tim Ferriss:** "The bottom line is that you need a 10x mindset. Exponential results require exponential thinking."

    - Promotes the idea that achieving extraordinary success requires extraordinary effort and thinking.

8. **Jeff Bezos:** "Work hard, have fun, make history."

    - Subtly promotes the idea of hard work being the primary factor in making history, which can overshadow the need for rest and health.

These quotes reflect a pervasive culture that often glorifies overwork and underestimates the importance of maintaining a healthy work-life balance. Some of them may resonate with you. You may have even heard one or more of them from your bosses or may even have said some of these things yourselves to others. Perhaps you noticed a commonality in them: the quotes are predominantly from men.

So, I searched for healthier quotes, ones that promoted a sustainable, ambitious, and perhaps a more responsible sense of hustle. Here are some inspiring quotes by women on sustainable ambition and the value of hard work:

1. **Hillary Clinton:** "Never doubt that you are valuable and powerful and deserving of every chance in the world to pursue your dreams."

2. **Ruth Bader Ginsburg:** "As women achieve power, the barriers will fall. As society sees what women can do, as women see what women can do, there will be more women out there doing things, and we'll all be better off for it."

3. **Sophie Brochu:** "Ambition is complex, it goes by many names, and has many faces. Ambition is the courage to live your life in your own way."

4. **Oprah Winfrey:** "Passion is energy. Feel the power that comes from focusing on what excites you."

5. **Marissa Mayer:** "I always did something I was a little not ready to do. I think that's how you grow. When there's that moment of 'Wow, I'm not really sure I can do this,' and you push through those moments, that's when you have a breakthrough."

6. **Beyoncé:** "We need to reshape our own perception of how we view ourselves. We have to step up as women and take the lead."

7. **Vandana Shiva:** "Real fulfillment comes from knowing you are of value to others."

8. **Cathy Onetto:** "Sustainable Ambition is about achieving success in a way that allows us to have a life, manage our energy, and avoid burning out, so we can keep going for the long haul, not just for a short burst."

These quotes highlight the balance between ambition and sustainability, emphasizing the importance of confidence, perseverance, and redefining success on one's own terms. They encourage a mindset that values hard work and resilience, while also recognizing the importance of self-belief and supportive environments.

The Masculine and Feminine Balance: Navigating Work, Family, and Burnout

Understanding the differences between how men and women approach work, driven by hormonal and brain distinctions, can be fascinating. Testosterone, the dominant hormone in men, fuels competitiveness, assertiveness, and a desire for dominance—traits often seen in risk-taking and leadership roles. It's like having a Spartan inside, cheering for every big project. On the other hand, women's higher levels of estrogen and oxytocin promote bonding, communication, and nurturing. These hormones encourage collaboration and empathy, as though a team of event planners is constantly organizing connection and cooperation.

Embracing these differences is key to fostering more harmonious workplaces but recognizing that both masculine and feminine energies are prone to similar traps—like overcommitting to work at the expense of personal life—transcends gender.

I'm reminded of a story I heard while preparing for a keynote with the police service that really hits home on the impact of giving everything to work and leaving little for home. It's about Winston a revered police officer known for his bravery and commitment. When he retired, his son, Colton, joined the service, proudly following in his father's footsteps. Colleagues showered Winston with praise, but for Colton, the hero at work wasn't the same man he knew at home. At home, Winston was always tired, barely present for family moments, missing out on birthdays and sporting events.

This story struck a personal chord. In many ways, I've been like Winston. As a working mom, I've juggled deadlines and family, convinced I was doing it all for them—only to realize I was missing out on what mattered most. The signs of burnout were there, but I chose to ignore them, like so many of us do. Winston's story reminds us that professional success comes with a cost if we aren't careful. I, too, received accolades and recognition at work, which felt great in the moment. But when I came home after long days, exhausted and mentally checked out, I missed those fleeting, precious moments with my kids. The handwritten notes from my daughter, apologizing for her behavior in the chaos of our mornings, broke my heart. She wasn't the problem—my mismanaged energy was. In chasing career goals, it's easy to lose sight of the moments that truly matter. We need to balance our legacy at work with our presence at home before we regret it. Because in the end, it's not the awards or promotions that define our legacy—it's the love, time, and memories we create with the people who mean the most.

Maladaptive Behaviors Are Celebrated

We have become great at glorifying the grind and promoting the hustle culture. During my research into it, I also went onto the busiest streets in Niagara Falls to interview people of all walks on their thoughts and experiences with hustle. Gathered one-liners sometimes, but most often advice from hundreds of my community members.

I received so many! I printed them all, cut them out, and posted them on my wall. I wanted to see how I could rearrange them and create something with them. But all I saw were contradictory messages. Messages that confuse, bewilder, and lead to burnout. No matter what order I put them in, they didn't line up. They didn't help or inspire. I made a video called "Hustle They Say," reading all the messages. Here's part of it: listen to see if any of this sounds familiar. We are flooded with these messages constantly. And just like the burnout corporate woman I used to be, I fight these messages still to this day.

Hustle they say.
Create your own life,

On your own terms.

Be your own boss.

Take on this extra project.

You should volunteer.

Make sure you take a vacation.

Give yourself a mental break.

Don't get too cozy.

Check your email in the afternoon.

Be responsive.

Wake up at five a.m.

Work out twenty minutes every day.

Follow the keto diet.

You should try the soup diet.

You look tired.

You can sleep when you're dead.

Take supplements.

Don't eat after eight p.m.

Get seven hours of good sleep.

Measure your heart rate.

Check your progress.

There's an app for that!

Your life needs to revolve around your work.

It doesn't work any other way.

Hustle they say.

Healthy and Unhealthy Awards

I nominated myself for an award that I was too burned out to actually receive. It's another personal story of hustling and burning out in my forties when I transitioned to another college. Once again, my workaholism and ambition overtook my capacity. Despite not being in the right state of mind, I pushed through and worked extra hard. I had an amazing colleague with whom I collaborated to develop entrepreneurial activities for our students. We were driven to bring something sustainable to the institution, recognizing that it was ready for such an initiative.

But it was a tough battle. In publicly funded models, things move very slowly, and we were used to a rapid pace and getting things done. This clash in work habits led to frustration and difficulties in being team players within the college. Despite the roadblocks and the "hurry up and wait" reactions, we pushed on, knowing that the impact we were making on students' lives was significant.

We decided to nominate ourselves for an award, feeling that our efforts deserved recognition that wasn't forthcoming from the institution. To our surprise, we won the President's Award for Innovation. While it was a big award from the college's perspective, for us it felt bittersweet. The recognition felt hollow without the institution's support along the way. It seemed the award was given more because of our compelling write-up and proof of concept than as a genuine acknowledgment of our efforts.

Neither of us was present to accept the award when it was given out, which further emphasized the disconnect we felt. We have the award, but it serves as a reminder of how we sought validation through external recognition, only to find it unfulfilling. It underscored the empty rewards of hustle culture, where the accolades don't compensate for the burnout and lack of genuine support. This experience highlights the need for healing ourselves and realigning our efforts with our true capacity and purpose. It's another example of how seeking validation through relentless work and external awards can leave us feeling more depleted than accomplished.

Enter the Healthy Hustle® Award.

I first decided to implement this award in the department I was working with at one of the big banks. They had hired me to work with them for eight weeks and teach them about capacity management strategies. I helped them with individual capacity management and team capacity building. The task was simple. After eight weeks of working together, we developed criteria to measure how people were showing up at work with intentions and behaviors that showcased wellness at work. We designed the Healthy Hustle criteria around behaviors at meetings, taking breaks, candid conversations with management and team members about workload, and so much more! The results were mind-blowing. The nomination statements were proof of productivity while taking care of one's health. The employee nominations were amazing to read through and witness how in little as eight weeks, team members could embrace a way of working that was sustainable but still ambitious. Here are a couple of examples of the nominations received:

Criteria: Nominee has motivated and encouraged others to maintain and improve their health and wellness while holding boundaries to keep themselves accountable.

"Ronnie is the Sr. Content Manager, and I was lucky enough to have him train me in my current role—I call him Coach Ron as he has been, and continues to be, an incredible resource in my position here at work. He always makes sure I can complete the tasks at hand, and coaches me when my capacity becomes a little stretched. He always puts our well-being first and books a weekly 1:1 to make sure our individual capacity is as achievable as possible—we work together to complete projects and even the workload. This safe and honest space is why we find as much success as we do in meeting our timelines."

Criteria: Nominee has held candid conversations when needing to push back on incremental requests.

"Ruby has been helping to fill a resource gap on our team since March, taking on two additional portfolios plus her existing ones. She's been very transparent about her capacity limitations and has been providing realistic expectations and respectfully challenging incremental asks coming from myself and her internal partners. An example is during our F23 planning cycle that is taking place—she and I divided up deliverables in order to deliver on time without putting further stress on her capacity."

Criteria: Nominee has demonstrated a full presence and participation at meetings while engaging with intention. They held "attention boundaries" without multitasking.

"Despite having to take on additional responsibilities, Xavier remained fully immersed and engaged during meetings. He is also on top of his required tasks without anything major falling through the cracks."

Incorporating a spirit of friendly competition within the workplace can significantly enhance accountability and foster a healthy capacity among team members. By introducing challenges that promote wellness and productivity, employees are motivated to push their limits in a balanced and supportive environment. This approach not only encourages personal and professional growth but also strengthens team cohesion as colleagues strive to achieve common goals. Friendly competition, when aligned with capacity management principles, can transform the workplace into a dynamic and invigorating space where everyone is inspired to excel, ensuring that they maintain optimal capacity without compromising their well-being.

When transitioning from the relentless demands of hustle culture, it's essential to explore the concept of resilience. While hustle culture glorifies constant productivity and unyielding effort, resilience embodies the capacity to recover and adapt amid challenges and setbacks. Understanding resilience allows us to shift our focus from merely surviving the grind to thriving despite adversity. By developing resilience, individuals can navigate the pressures of modern work life more sustainably, ultimately fostering a healthier balance and greater long-term success.

Chapter Nine

From Stress to Strength: Crossing the Threshold of Resilience

The barrier to resiliency is stress. When stress becomes detrimental, we cross the threshold into "distress." — Dr. Robyne Hanley-Dafoe

Diary Entry

I'm testing my resilience.

Starving my ego.

Releasing capacity, reserved only for fear.

Old fears. Doubts. Self-preservation.

Deep excuses and old justifications creep in, trying to persuade you of every reason imaginable for why it is a terrible idea.

It's the fear of the unknown. Fear of being uncomfortable. Fear of a mistake. Fear of being wrong. Fear of someone mocking you.

Did you know you have capacity that holds courage?

I double-dog dare you to access it today.

What old and heavy capacity can you release to move forward with?

A colleague. A boss. A project. A conversation. A family member. A decision that desperately needs to be made.

A Story of True Resilience: Turning Adversity into Opportunity

One of the most impactful people I met from the entrepreneurship incubator that I founded at an Ontario college was Abhishek, a student from Gujarat, India, who has since become a close friend. His story exemplifies resilience, self-belief, and the power of pursuing a dream, no matter how impossible it may seem.

When Abhishek joined the program, he had an audacious goal: to launch a mobile leasing business aimed at international students and others seeking the latest phones without being tied to lengthy contracts. The idea seemed almost impossible, given the dominance of major telecom companies in Canada. But Abhishek saw something the rest of us didn't—an overlooked gap in the mobile industry.

In addition to leasing phones, he planned to sell accessories and offer repair services, which, while common ideas individually, became ingenious when paired with his mobile leasing model. This service filled a critical gap for international students who arrived in Canada without a Social Insurance Number or established credit. Abhishek worked tirelessly, even partnering with mobile service providers to ensure his customers had the services they needed.

At first, his pitch was met with resistance. Investors and mentors doubted him, and the feedback was filled with skepticism. Despite facing constant rejection and a lack of support, Abhishek remained undeterred. He believed in his vision so deeply that he enrolled in another program just to stay in Canada and keep working toward his dream, even though he was already well educated in India. Abhishek's journey was anything but smooth. He refused financial support from his parents, determined to do it all on his own. He faced setbacks, was burned by several business partners, and battled discrimination, racism, and the inherent challenges that come with being an international student trying to start a business. But through it all, he never gave up.

That's when our incubator and entrepreneurial community stepped in. We saw his determination and believed in his potential, and offered the support he needed. Today, I'm proud to say that Abhishek's business has a permanent location at the college where it all began. He has since expanded to three additional locations and is thriving both personally and professionally. He is now a permanent resident of Canada, has purchased a home, and continues to succeed in every aspect of his life.

I'm not just proud of what Abhishek has achieved but of what he's shown us all about resilience, self-belief, and sticking to your values. Even when the odds were against him, he led with grace and gratitude. His story is a powerful reminder that with perseverance, belief, and a supportive community, dreams can indeed become reality.

Embracing Resilience

As part of my research, I had the opportunity to interview the amazing Dr. Robyne Hanley-Dafoe. She is a seasoned speaker and writer, and an expert on the topic of resilience. Her approach goes beyond merely discussing bouncing back from adversity. Dr. Hanley-Dafoe's journey into resilience began with a realization: it's not enough to tough it out. Instead, she focuses on fostering wellness as a foundation for true resilience. By addressing stressors, traumas, and losses, she guides individuals and teams toward not just surviving but excelling in both personal and professional spheres. Dr. Hanley-Dafoe's authenticity resonates deeply with her audience, particularly her willingness to share her vulnerabilities. Despite her successful academic career, she openly acknowledges her past struggles, including dropping out of high school and overcoming learning disabilities. This transparency fosters connection and inspires hope, showing that setbacks need not define one's trajectory.

One pivotal moment came when she decided to embrace her personal story fully. Despite warnings of academic repercussions, she chose to integrate her personal narrative with her research, culminating in her book *Calm Within the Storm*. This bold move marked a shift from fearing judgment to embracing authenticity, a journey toward resilience in its truest form.

Dr. Hanley-Dafoe's insights extend to the pervasive culture of hustle, where perseverance is often mistaken for resilience. She distinguishes between adaptive and maladaptive behaviors, challenging the notion that relentless work is the key to success. True resilience, she asserts, lies in finding balance, recognizing when to persist and when to pause for self-care. In her view, resilience isn't a destination but a continuous journey of self-discovery and growth. By prioritizing wellness, aligning actions with values, and embracing vulnerability, individuals can cultivate resilience that empowers them to thrive in the face of adversity.

Teaching Resilience to Teenagers

My husband and I are part of the coaching staff for a high-level girls' basketball team composed of fourteen- and fifteen-year-olds. We focus specifically on mindset development. Coaching adolescent girls means dealing with a myriad of unpredictable factors—hair, hormones, social dynamics, school pressures, and general drama. Each practice and game can present a new set of challenges, so we emphasize the importance of mastering their mindset.

Over the past two years, we've concentrated on helping these athletes control their emotions. We coined the acronym LIFT (Locked In, Intentional, Focused, and Together) to remind them of what is crucial during games. Initially, our team struggled in the third quarter, consistently losing momentum, which made the final quarter even more of a struggle. To address this, we introduced the concept of "alter egos," inspired by Todd Herman. We encouraged the girls to envision themselves differently on the court than their school or home personas. This transformative approach helped them adopt a more competitive and resilient mindset during games.

Additionally, we incorporated visualization techniques, having the girls mentally rehearse various on-court scenarios, focusing on how they would perform and react. We also discussed the idea of peaks and valleys, teaching them how to access and practice resilience. This resilience training, informed by the work of Dr. Hanley-Dafoe, highlighted the fact that resilience is not innate but a skill to be cultivated daily. Following the implementation of the strategies, the young athletes experienced a significant transformation both in their individual performances and in overall team dynamics. By reconnecting with their core values, the team was able to strengthen their collective focus and morale. This realignment served as a powerful foundation, enabling them to navigate the challenges they faced with greater clarity and confidence.

Additionally, the team honed in on the four critical areas of focus (LIFT), which became their key performance drivers. This allowed them to improve their outcomes, even when they encountered setbacks. The ability to narrow down priorities to a few essential tasks proved invaluable, a strategy that anyone can apply to enhance their effectiveness and reduce overwhelm under pressure.

Finally, the increased resilience displayed by the team, particularly when faced with adversity, highlights the importance of not just bouncing back but also leveraging challenges to foster growth. The principles they embraced became even more effective in tough times, pushing them to persevere and succeed.

Strategies for Resilience

To truly understand and embrace resilience, it's essential to move beyond the conventional notion of simply "bouncing back." During the conversation on my podcast with Dr. Hanley-Dafoe Hanley-Defoe, she posed a thought-provoking question that resonated deeply: *Is resilience merely about the speed at which we recover after facing adversity?* She suggests otherwise. It's not how quickly we rebound but rather the decisions we make amid chaos and crisis, the behaviors we exhibit when life tests us.

Resilience entails more than just speed—it requires strategies to ground ourselves when faced with overwhelming challenges. We have to return to our core, our center, in the midst of life's storms. We often think of resilience as something we have to master under pressure, but like building physical strength, resilience is cultivated through consistent practice. It's the accumulation of small, intentional actions we take every day in response to adversity that strengthens our resilience muscles. Having a system or set of practices in place helps reassure us that, despite the difficulties, we will emerge on the other side with clarity and strength.

Dr. Hanley-Dafoe's insights offer a great roadmap for anyone seeking to navigate life's tumultuous terrain with grace and poise. Resilience isn't just surviving—it's thriving through the peaks of achievement and persevering through the valleys of adversity. And in doing so, we discover the transformative power that resilience has to shape a more fulfilling life journey. It goes beyond bouncing back; it's evolving, growing, and ultimately emerging stronger and more hopeful after each challenge.

Resilience, then, isn't merely an innate trait that some are born with and others are not. It's a skill—one that can be nurtured and developed over time. Built on a foundation of inner strength, resilience thrives when supported by a sense of purpose, positive relationships, and a balanced perspective on life. It's enhanced when we show gratitude and kindness and practice self-compassion, fortifying our ability to navigate the complexities of life and transforming adversity into opportunities for growth and renewal.

So, as you reflect on your own journey, consider this: how are you cultivating your resilience? What daily practices or systems do you have in place to bring yourself back to center when life gets overwhelming? How do you respond—not just in the moments of crisis, but in the small, quiet moments when you can choose to build strength for the road ahead? Whether you find yourself in the rapid currents of change or in the slow, meandering flow of everyday life, resilience isn't just what *gets us through*—it's what helps us *grow through*.

As Dr. Hanley-Defoe often emphasizes that resilience requires progress but not perfection. It's the cumulative effect of small actions that help you return to your center when life feels overwhelming. She advocates focusing on what you can control, embracing imperfection, and practicing self-compassion—actions that also help optimize your capacity. To build both resilience and capacity, she suggests creating a "resilience bank" by regularly engaging in practices that support mental, emotional, and physical well-being. By making daily deposits into this bank—whether through reflection, mindfulness, or rest—you'll be better equipped to handle challenges with renewed capacity and inner strength. By blending these concepts of resilience and capacity optimization, you'll not only improve your ability to manage adversity but also cultivate a balanced, sustainable approach to life that honors your overall well-being.

But wait, there's more! Just when I thought Dr. Hanley-Dafoe had written *the* book on resilience, her second one, *Stressing Wisely*, completely blew me away. In it she redefines how we think about stress—not as something to be feared or avoided, but as something we can manage and even harness for growth. *Stressing Wisely* invites readers to reconsider their relationship with stress, offering practical strategies to help navigate life's pressures in healthier, more intentional ways.

One of the standout concepts in the book is the idea that not all stress is harmful. Dr. Hanley-Dafoe helps readers identify which stressors can be managed and which need to be let go. She breaks down the difference between healthy stress, which motivates us and drives growth, and chronic, harmful stress that leads to burnout. By learning how to "stress wisely," we can better manage our energy, prioritize what truly matters, and ultimately cultivate resilience in both our personal and professional lives. The book includes actionable tools for managing stress through mindfulness, reframing challenges, and creating intentional recovery periods, emphasizing the importance of recognizing when to push forward and when to step back, and giving ourselves permission to rest and reset without guilt.

The *5 Second Rule*

As we explore strategies to cultivate resilience, one simple yet powerful tool to add to your resilience toolkit is Mel Robbins's *5 Second Rule*. Robbins introduces this playful approach in her book, which leverages the brain's natural response to hesitation. The rule is simple: count down from five, and then take immediate action. This countdown disrupts the cycle of overthinking and self-doubt, propelling us forward into motion before our brain has a chance to talk us out of it. In this way, it fosters resilience by encouraging a proactive stance in the face of challenges, making quick decision-making and courageous action habitual.

In one of her short stories, Robbins recounts a moment when she used the 5 Second Rule to overcome her fear of public speaking. Paralyzed with anxiety and fear moments before stepping onto the stage, she counted down from five and propelled herself into action. That small but significant victory was the turning point—she transformed fear into forward motion. It's a perfect example of how resilience can be built in increments, through small moments of courage where we choose action over hesitation.

I know that feeling well.

It was one of those mornings where getting out of bed felt like trying to summit Mount Everest—in flip-flops. My alarm had long given up, and I was cocooned in the warmth of my blankets, contemplating every life decision that led me to this moment of profound inertia. But then I remembered Robbins and her magical 5 Second Rule.

"Alright, brain, let's play a game," I muttered to myself, hoping to muster some enthusiasm. "You versus me. I count down from five, and if I'm not out of bed by then, you win. But if I am, I win. And we both know who likes winning more." With the challenge set, I took a deep breath and began the countdown.

"Five!" I shouted, startling my eighty-five-pound bernadoodle at the foot of my bed.

"Four!" My eyes fluttered open.

"Three!" My legs twitched in anticipation.

"Two!" My arms stretched out, ready to push myself up.

"One!" With a burst of energy, I flung the blankets off and leapt out of bed like a superhero ready to save the day.

Standing triumphantly on the floor, I couldn't help but laugh at the absurdity of it all. My brain had tried every trick to keep me under those blankets, but the playful countdown turned the struggle into a game I was determined to win. That small victory left me feeling victorious and energized, transforming what could have been a sluggish, uninspired morning into one filled with a renewed sense of resilience. All thanks to a simple, playful tool that helped me take action when I least wanted to.

This moment encapsulates an important truth about resilience: it doesn't always apply to grand gestures or life-altering events. It's often built in these small moments of personal triumph when we choose to take action, despite the pull of comfort or fear. Whether it's using the 5 Second Rule to jump out of bed, take the stage, or confront a difficult situation, these small actions strengthen our resilience, reminding us that we are capable of more than we give ourselves credit for. So, as you reflect on your own resilience practices, consider adopting this simple rule. When you feel hesitation creeping in or the weight of indecision holding you back, try counting down from five and pushing yourself into action. Over time, this practice can become a powerful tool, helping you face challenges with confidence and build resilience incrementally—one small victory at a time.

Resilience and Capacity Reflection Exercise: Strengthen Your Inner Reserves

When you build resilience, you learn to bounce back and to optimize your capacity to manage life's challenges with grace and strength. In this exercise, we'll explore how your resilience practices can enhance and expand your personal capacity for growth, energy, and balance.

Step 1: Reflect on Your Recent Challenges

Think of a recent situation that tested your resilience. It could be something small, like managing a difficult day, or something larger, like handling a significant change or setback. Answer and write down:

- What was the challenge or adversity?

- How did it impact your mental, emotional, or physical capacity?

- What actions did you take to manage the situation?

Step 2: Identify Your Resilience Tools

Consider the strategies you used to help you bounce back or regain balance. Did you lean on your support network, use mindfulness techniques, or employ something like Mel Robbins's 5 Second Rule to help navigate through the challenge? Answer and write down:

- What specific resilience practices did I use in this situation?

- How did they help me restore or conserve my capacity?

- Were there any missed opportunities where I could have used a resilience tool or practice to better manage my energy?

Step 3: Build Your "Capacity Net Worth"

Dr. Hanley-Dafoe writes about the "resilience bank," where you make regular, intentional deposits that support your mental, emotional, and physical well-being. These daily practices help ensure you have reserves to draw upon when life gets difficult. Now, think about how you can build your capacity net worth by consistently making deposits. For each area of your capacity (Purpose, Energy, and Connection), identify one or two small actions you can incorporate daily or weekly:

- *Purpose:* Actions that align with your core purpose and long-term goals, helping you stay focused and motivated in times of challenge.

  ○ Example: Reflect each morning on how today's tasks contribute to your larger purpose or take one step toward a goal that is meaningful to you.

- *Energy:* Practices that help restore and maintain your physical and emotional energy, ensuring you have the strength to face challenges and maintain resilience.

  ○ Example: Prioritize rest and recovery by setting a consistent bedtime or incorporating short breaks throughout the day to recharge.

- *Connection:* Actions that nurture your relationships and sense of community, both with others and with yourself, to help you draw strength from meaningful interactions.

  ○ Example: Reach out to someone for a meaningful conversation or practice self-compassion by reflecting on your feelings and experiences through journaling.

By focusing on your Purpose, Energy, and Connection, you'll strengthen your capacity and resilience, equipping yourself to manage challenges with clarity and grace. Consistently depositing into your resilience bank is an investment in your future, ensuring you have the reserves needed when challenges arise. Remember, resilience and capacity are built through regular, intentional practice, creating a solid foundation to draw upon when you need it most.

Resilience has been a lifelong practice for me, necessitated by the myriad barriers, traps, and subconscious inner workings that would otherwise hinder my daily progress. Grief, trauma, fear of missing out, and people-pleasing are just a few of the challenges I've had to navigate. To overcome these, I've had to continuously work on my resilience, much like strengthening a muscle. It involves pushing boundaries, speaking up despite fear, planning ahead, and tackling difficult challenges head-on rather than seeking the easy way out.

Every day, in both my personal and professional life, I must remain vigilant and practice resilience. Embracing this as a lifelong endeavor has been a profound realization for me. It's also become one of the most powerful tools in my toolkit, one on which I can always rely. This commitment to resilience, despite the difficulties, has been a key aspect of my journey and continues to be a major success factor in my life. Furthermore, resilience equips me to handle difficult conversations with poise and clarity, ensuring that I can navigate through challenging dialogues with the same steadfastness that has guided me through other adversities.

Chapter Ten

The Weight of Words: Healing Through Vulnerability and Honest Conversations

The hardest truths are the ones that will ultimately set us free.
The discomfort we feel during those conversations is where growth
begins. — Laura Gassner Otting

Diary Entry

*T*elling people I'm struggling is bittersweet.

The sweet part is that it feels good to tell a few trusted people. Their love and care shine through as they want to chat, help, and show support.

But the bitter part is that I can't accept their help right now. It's too hard. I'm too unstable.

I remember being on the other side, wanting to help, to talk someone out of their feelings, to make them right again, to take away their pain, crack jokes, and move on. Just get over it.

But being on this side is like facing an eerily familiar unknown. I can predict where this will go, which almost makes me feel like I should be fine, but I'm not.

It's a mind trick.

I'm predicting, maybe even preparing for, things to be rocky between my partner and me. He will probably bear the brunt of this, but he won't be able to ease my mind or support me like he has in the past.

This isn't a sore arm, a cold, a sprained ankle, or even a bruised ego. It's a broken spirit, a depleted mental state that will take time and work to heal. This is the unpredictable diagnosis.

I don't know how long this will take. I don't even know what type of therapy this will require. But I know my soul is cracked. Badly.

The Time I Tried to Write a TEDx with My Therapist

I was a year and a half into therapy, diagnosed with depression, and dealing with full burnout. Despite this, I was finding my way back—reconnecting with my purpose, healing my energy, and strengthening relationships. Things were looking up.

Then, I got an invitation to do my second TEDx talk. My mind exploded with ideas—burnout, healing, recovery—it was all so relevant! I thought, 'This is the universe giving me a platform to share my journey!' My brain kicked into overdrive. I had a plan. And who better to co-create it with than my therapist?

Yes, you heard that right. I decided I would co-write a TEDx talk with my therapist. Genius, right? My plan was full of excitement, and I just knew she would jump on board. I imagined us brainstorming and fleshing out this brilliant talk about burnout—while I was still deeply in it.

So there I was, about to unleash my grand TEDx idea. I'm excited, and she's prepared to support my healing. And then, after listening to me ramble, she stopped me and said, "Given where you are in your healing journey, how do you think taking on another TEDx talk would impact your progress and well-being?"

In that moment, I had to confront the reality of my functioning burnout. The FOMO was real. I wanted to honor the invitation, convinced I could somehow manage it. But that's what burnout does—it convinces you that you can do it all, even when you can barely keep up. It took my therapist's question to remind me: protecting my capacity was far more important than chasing another shiny opportunity.

Vulnerability and Burnout

In her book *Daring Greatly*, Brené Brown explores the profound impact of vulnerability on our lives, particularly in the context of work and personal fulfillment. Brown identifies vulnerability as a crucial element in combating burnout.

She argues that acknowledging our limitations and embracing vulnerability can lead to more authentic and resilient lives.

Some of her key insights on vulnerability and burnout are:

1. **The Power of Connection:** Connection is a fundamental human need and building meaningful relationships can provide a buffer against burnout. Being open about our struggles and seeking support can foster deeper connections and shared resilience.

2. **Setting Boundaries:** Setting boundaries is critically important. Saying no and setting limits are acts of self-care that protect against overcommitment and exhaustion. Boundaries help individuals maintain their energy and focus on what truly matters to them.

3. **"Shame Resilience":** Shame resilience allows you to recognize and address feelings of shame rather than letting them fester. Shame often contributes to burnout by making individuals feel isolated and inadequate. Building resilience to shame involves practicing self-compassion, reaching out for support, and speaking about one's experiences.

4. **Cultivating Self-compassion:** Practicing self-compassion is essential for preventing burnout. This means treating oneself with the same kindness and understanding that one would offer to a friend. Self-compassion helps in acknowledging imperfections and moving forward without self-criticism.

5. **Authenticity:** Living authentically, true to your values and beliefs, reduces the risk of burnout. When individuals align their actions with their values, they experience less internal conflict and greater fulfillment, making them more resilient to stress.

Brené Brown's insights on vulnerability and resilience align with the components of purpose and connection in the capacity management framework. By embracing vulnerability, individuals can become more aware of their true needs and values, leading to more intentional and sustainable commitments. Setting boundaries and practicing self-compassion are practical applications that support the framework's goal of managing capacity effectively.

Vulnerability and Healing

Rosaline

A client of mine named Rosaline was a successful project manager at a renowned tech firm, known for her ability to juggle multiple tasks and meet tight deadlines. On the outside, Rosaline appeared to have it all together, but inside she was battling the silent storm of burnout. Her days were a whirlwind of meetings, emails, and constant demands. She prided herself on being the go-to person, the one who never said no. However, the weight of her responsibilities began to take a toll. Her energy waned, and the spark that once fueled her passion dimmed. She found herself feeling disconnected, not only from her work but from her loved ones as well.

One evening, after a particularly grueling day, Rosaline sat alone in her apartment, feeling the full weight of her exhaustion. In a moment of clarity, she remembered Brené Brown's book. Desperate for a way out of her despair, she began to read. Brown's words resonated deeply with Rosaline. Feeling inspired, she made a decision. The next morning, she walked into her boss's office and, with a trembling voice, shared her struggles. She admitted that she was overwhelmed and on the brink of burnout. To her surprise, her boss listened with empathy and understanding. Instead of seeing Rosaline's vulnerability as a weakness, he saw it as a courageous act of honesty.

With her boss's support, Rosaline was able to delegate some of her responsibilities and take time off to recharge. She used this time to reconnect with herself and her passions. She began attending yoga classes, spending time in nature, and reconnecting with friends and family. Each step towards self-care was a step towards healing. Rosaline's journey wasn't easy. There were moments when she doubted herself, moments when the weight of vulnerability felt excruciating. But slowly, she began to feel a shift. By embracing her vulnerability, she discovered a resilience she never knew she had. She learned that it's ok to ask for help and that admitting our struggles can open the door to deeper connections and authentic support.

When Rosaline returned to work, she brought with her a new perspective. She was more mindful of her limits and more compassionate towards herself and others. Her willingness to be vulnerable had not only helped her heal but had also fostered a culture of openness and empathy within her team. In the end, Rosaline found that the act of being vulnerable, though painful, led to profound healing. She realized that true strength lies in the courage to be vulnerable. As Brené Brown has so wisely written, "Vulnerability is not winning or losing; it's having the courage to show up and be seen when we have no control over the outcome."

And so, Rosaline continued to show up, embracing her vulnerability and living a more authentic, resilient life.

Me

Having tough conversations has been a significant part of my journey toward growth and healing. Vulnerability, which once seemed like a weakness, has proven to be my superpower. These challenging dialogues have fortified my resilience and boosted my confidence.

I vividly remember moments in my marriage when I was ready to walk away. I recall sitting with my husband, feeling as if I were about to confess a profound truth: our marriage wasn't working, and I wasn't happy. The look of sheer hurt and disappointment on his face will stay with me forever. It felt to him like this revelation came out of nowhere. He knew I wasn't happy, but he didn't realize the extent of it. The truth was, my unhappiness wasn't because of him. It was the external pressures, stress, and shame from other aspects of my life that had seeped into our relationship. I was exhausted, and plagued by self-defeatism, and these negative emotions created a wedge between us.

It wasn't his fault, yet I had mistakenly placed the blame on our marriage. Through deep conversations, reflection, and giving each other space, I came to understand that our marriage wasn't the root of the problem. Instead, it highlighted the need for us to dream together, support each other, and move beyond merely coexisting as two highly ambitious individuals and devoted parents.

Often, stress can distort our perceptions, leading us to misplace blame on those closest to us. I am eternally grateful for the opportunity to have those difficult conversations and for the patience we found to realize that the issues stemmed from deep-rooted subconscious programming. It required healing and space and tough discussions to understand how to work together and overcome the challenges. Through this process, we learned that vulnerability isn't a weakness but a path to deeper connection and resilience.

How LGO Gave Me Permission to Be a Mediocre Mom

Stress and burnout can infiltrate adult relationships, but can also affect the (unrealistic) expectations of how I am supposed to be a good mother.

The following is a brief summary of my interview with LGO (aka Laura Gassner Otting), best-selling author of *Limitless* and *Wonderhell*. I was fortunate enough to have her as a guest on my podcast. She is bright, vivacious, and one of the best storytellers I've had the pleasure of sitting with. However, I wanted to share an important piece of our conversation. The passage below is when she gave me permission to be a mediocre mom or entrepreneur: I had to pick one because I couldn't be exceptional at both. She had managed to silence the inner functioning burnout's voice.

Mel: Let's dive right in. You often talk about your calling and how it evolves over time. Can you tell us more about that?

LGO: Absolutely. I believe that our calling isn't a fixed destination but rather a journey that changes as we grow and our circumstances evolve. Early in my career, my calling was all about building a successful business and making a mark in my industry. I was driven and tenacious, always pushing myself to achieve more. But as I progressed, I realized that my personal life, especially my role as a parent, also needed attention and revaluation.

Mel: That's fascinating. How did this intense focus on work impact your family life?

LGO: Well, it's a bit of a double-edged sword. My work habits and mentality, which were incredibly effective in a professional setting, didn't translate well to family life. I was so used to driving hard for results, setting high expectations, and being relentless in my pursuits. These traits made me exceptional at work but not necessarily a great fit for parenting. I found myself being what some might call a "mediocre mom."

Mel: That's a bold admission. Can you elaborate on what you mean by being a "mediocre mom"?

LGO: Sure. By "mediocre mom" I mean that I wasn't meeting the often unrealistic standards society sets for what a "perfect" mother should be. I wasn't always present at every school event, I didn't bake cookies for the bake sales, and sometimes I missed bedtime stories because I was finishing a project or taking a business call. In the eyes of society, that made me a mediocre parent. But I had to accept that I couldn't be exceptional in all areas of my life at the same time.

Mel: It sounds like you're saying there's a trade-off between being exceptional at work and being a parent.

LGO: Exactly. My work habits and mentality—being a driver, being tenacious, never settling for anything less than the best—were crucial for my success in the professional world. But applying those same principles at home didn't always work. Family life requires a different approach, one that values presence over performance, patience over persistence. It was a tough realization, but an important one.

Mel: How did you come to terms with this realization?

LGO: It was a gradual process. I had to reframe my thinking and accept that being a "mediocre mom" in the traditional sense didn't mean I was failing my children. Instead, I chose to focus on the quality of the time I spent with them, rather than the quantity. I embraced the idea that I could be a role model in a different way—by showing them the importance of pursuing one's passion and being dedicated to one's work while still making room for family.

Mel: That's a powerful perspective. Society often pressures us to excel in all areas, making it seem like there's something wrong with prioritizing one over the other.

LGO: Exactly. Society tells us that we need to be perfect parents, perfect professionals, and perfect partners all at once. But that's an impossible standard. There's nothing wrong with being exceptional at work and accepting that you might not meet all the traditional expectations of parenthood. What's important is finding a balance that works for you and your family, and being honest about your limitations.

Mel: Thank you for sharing that. It's refreshing to hear such an honest take on balancing work and family life.

LGO: My pleasure. I hope it helps others understand that it's ok to be imperfect and to embrace their unique journey, whatever that may look like.

This conversation with LGO highlights the evolving nature of one's calling, the challenges of balancing work and family life, and the importance of embracing vulnerability and imperfection. It underscores the idea that societal expectations can often be unrealistic, and finding a personal balance is key to fulfillment and resilience.

Coping Ahead

One method I find extremely helpful in keeping my high-demand commitments in check with less guilt is having a coping strategy. Coping ahead involves proactively preparing yourself, your family, and your environment for an anticipated period of intense work. This means clearly communicating with your loved ones about the upcoming demands on your time and energy, setting realistic expectations, and creating a support system to manage household responsibilities and emotional needs. By organizing your workspace, planning meals in advance, and arranging for additional childcare or household help if needed, you can alleviate some of the stress associated with long workdays. Establishing routines and boundaries ensures that while you are immersed in your work, your family feels supported and understood, fostering a collaborative and resilient atmosphere that can endure the temporary intensity.

Moments of high stress distort the problem and if we don't approach them with an open heart ready to give and receive, we'll always be taking one step forward and two steps back. The truth of the matter is that we don't always know how to respond. Our emotions take over and we start shooting from the hip like a wild cowboy or cowgirl or we simply cower in the corner. These are instinctive, built-in self-preservation techniques. However, along the way I've discovered that practicing resilience and self-control have helped me in many situations.

Below are scenarios that may instigate uncontrolled emotional responses. I've included a few examples that will allow you to respond from a vulnerably confident position.

Responding Scenarios

Managers

Request – Manager: "Can you take on this additional project? It's a high priority."

Response – Employee: "I appreciate the importance of this project. Currently, I don't have the capacity to take on more work without compromising the quality of my existing commitments. Could we discuss reprioritizing my current tasks or extending the deadline?"

Family Members

Request - Family Member: "Can you help organize the family reunion next month?"

Response – You: "I love the idea of a family reunion, but right now I don't have the capacity to take on more responsibilities. Maybe we can delegate tasks among more family members or plan it for a less busy time?"

Friends

Request – Friend: "Can you join us for a weekend getaway next month?"

Response – You: "That sounds like a lot of fun! Unfortunately, I don't have the capacity for a weekend trip at the moment due to other commitments. Let's plan something for later in the year when things are less hectic."

External Requests to Be on Committees

Request – Committee Chair: "We would love for you to join our committee. Your input would be invaluable."

Response – You: "I'm honored by the invitation, and I believe in the committee's mission. However, I don't have the capacity to commit fully currently. Please keep me in mind for future opportunities when I might be able to contribute more effectively."

Extra Work Tasks

Request – Colleague: "Can you cover my shift this weekend? I have an emergency."

Response – You: "I understand your situation and I wish I could help. Unfortunately, I don't have the capacity to take on extra shifts right now without it affecting my own work-life balance."

Additional Responsibilities at Work

Request – Supervisor: "Can you lead the new training program for our team?"

Response – You: "I'm flattered that you considered me for this role. However, I don't have the capacity to take on additional responsibilities right now. I want to ensure I can perform my current duties to the best of my abilities."

Volunteer Requests

Request – Volunteer Coordinator: "We need extra hands for the charity event next week. Can you help?"

Response – You: "I really support the cause, but at the moment, I don't have the capacity to volunteer. I hope the event goes well, and I can help in other ways when I have more availability."

Social Invitations

Request – Friend: "Can you come to my birthday party this Saturday?"

Response – You: "Happy early birthday! I would love to celebrate with you, but I don't have the capacity for social events this weekend. Let's catch up another time soon."

These examples illustrate how "I don't have the capacity for that" acknowledges the request's importance while clearly communicating your current limits. Practicing vulnerability builds your resilience. It is like removing a heavy mask that you've worn for years. It allows you to breathe freely and see the world clearly, fostering deeper connections with those around you. By sharing your authentic self, fears, and imperfections, you create space for genuine relationships built on trust and empathy. Vulnerability acts as the fertile soil in which personal growth and resilience take root, leading to a more fulfilling and balanced life. Just as a tree needs to shed its leaves to grow anew, embracing vulnerability enables you to let go of pretense and embrace the strength found in your true self.

This page is intentionally left blank for you to capture some notes, thoughts, and reflections on what we've covered in Part 2: Optimize Your Capacity.

PART 3: HONOR YOUR CAPACITY

Chapter Eleven

Egocake: Savor the Layers of Life without Overload

I've learned that you can't have everything and do everything at the same time. — Oprah Winfrey

Diary Entry

I had an interesting conversation with my mom today.

Mom: *"Wow, Mel, your life looks like this decadent and beautiful dessert table. Filled with an array of mouth-watering desserts."*

Mel: *"Thanks, yes, I have quite the project list on the go! Busy busy!"*

Mom: *"And you have taken a bite out of every single one."*

Mel: *Not what I was expecting, I thought.* "Sure." *I nodded slowly and hesitantly and responded:* "Yes, I guess I have."

Mom: *"I have a question for you."*

Mel: *Uh-oh, here it comes, I thought.*

Mom: *"Which one of these desserts have you loved the most?"*

Me: *Speechless. No words were able to leave my mouth.*

The Making of Egocake: A Delicious Capacity Framework

This was a conversation that I will never forget because I realized she was right. I was bloated with my own commitments. I had overfilled my plate with too many obligations and was unable to appreciate any of them, believing I had all the time in the world to get it all done. A delusion. So later that week, I created a framework called Egocake with the intention to deconstruct commitment habits while improving your daily life and work, bringing more focus, energy, and purpose to everything you do.

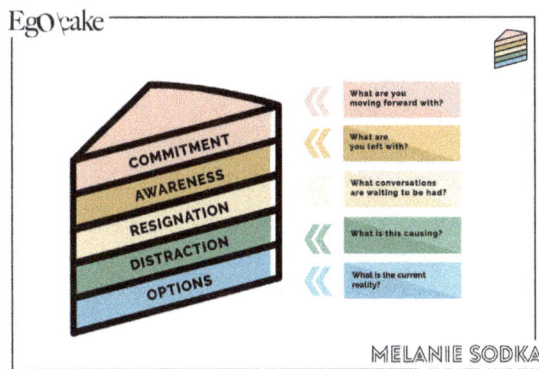

Figrue 11.1 The Egocake Framework

The framework (figure 11.1) is a five-layer framework designed to help individuals and teams manage their commitments and enhance their well-being:

1. Options: addresses the overwhelm caused by too many choices, encouraging prioritization

2. Distraction: focuses on minimizing disruptions to boost productivity

3. Resignation: involves letting go of commitments that no longer serve you

4. Awareness: emphasizes understanding your current reality and needs

5. Commitment: promotes making thoughtful and purposeful commitments

Together, these layers work to prevent burnout and foster a more focused, energized, and connected approach to personal and professional life.

The Struggle to Admit You're Overloaded

These unaligned commitments which produce unfulfillment are hard on our mental health. They take a toll, like trying to walk on a broken foot without letting it heal first. Unlike a physical injury that is visible and allows for observable progress during rehabilitation, mental health challenges like mental illness, breakdowns, fatigue, burnout, and paranoia are often invisible. When you express that you're struggling, there's an implicit expectation for you to be consistently and visibly incapacitated, so that (continuing the analogy) people can see that the cast on your foot prevents you from being able to walk. There is no room for deviation or nuance in the obviousness of your incapacity.

However, with mental health issues, your mind can fluctuate dramatically within the same day. You can experience moments of clarity and joy (the cast is off), followed by periods of intense struggle (the cast is back on). Those good moments might signal to others that you are fully healed, that you are back to normal because your cast has been removed. This creates a paradox. The fleeting clarity and joy become sources of paranoia and guilt because once you've disclosed your reduced mental and emotional capacity, you attach a stigma to yourself. It's as if you're constantly waiting for someone to accuse you of faking your struggles. If you laugh or smile, it looks like proof to others that you're not suffering, leading you to a profound sense of guilt and fear of judgment.

This stigma perpetuates a harmful cycle. You feel terrible and guilty when joy appears, despite knowing that it's natural to find humor and laughter even amidst suffering. Displaying any joy often leads others to assume that you're fully capable of managing your responsibilities and even taking on more. This can create an expectation that you're able to overextend yourself despite any internal struggles. Meanwhile, your own mind might undermine these joyful moments, making you feel like a fraud or an attention seeker for experiencing happiness amidst your challenges. This enforces the harmful notion that laughter and joy are incompatible with mental health struggles, further perpetuating the overwhelming myth that you must always be fully in control of your time and capabilities.

Despite our constant drive to squeeze more productivity out of each day, our gadgets and apps often intensify the feeling that there's never enough time. We become trapped in a cycle of busyness, striving for efficiency yet finding ourselves more overwhelmed than ever. But what if, instead of fixating on time management, we turned our attention to the deeper, more transformative idea of capacity? This shift in perspective could open new doors, leading us not just to better time use, but to a richer, more intentional way of living. With this in mind, let's explore a social experiment involving Egocake, where participants are invited to choose their own "desserts" and, in doing so, redefine what it means to truly savor life's moments.

A Social Experiment

At the start of my sessions, I love to kick things off with a fun icebreaker that also serves as a sneaky introduction to the Egocake framework. Picture this: a massive array of desserts—cupcakes, brownies, macarons, you name it—all beautiful, tasty, and designed to tempt even the most disciplined eater. What the participants don't know is that this dessert buffet is about to reveal a lot about their decision-making styles.

As the attendees file in, I watch the magic unfold. There's always *The Tower Builder* who piles their plate so high with desserts that it's a small engineering marvel. They're clearly ready for anything life (or the dessert table) throws at them. Then there's *The Single-Minded* one who zeroes in on one perfect dessert, ignoring all other options, like a dessert-seeking missile. Their focus is both impressive and slightly terrifying. Next, we have *The Sampler*. They return with a modest selection—two or three different desserts. It's a balanced approach, a nod to their careful consideration. They want to taste everything, but not overindulge. And finally, there's *The Indecisive* one. They linger at the table, looking at every option multiple times, possibly consulting a dessert oracle, and are always the last to return to their seat with a small, hesitantly chosen selection.

Once everyone is settled, I ask them to share what they chose. The responses are as varied as the desserts themselves. But the real fun begins when I ask them how they made their decisions. This question usually elicits some thoughtful pauses and a few nervous chuckles.

The Tower Builder admits they couldn't decide, so they just took everything. Cue the indulgence state for capacity and perhaps a hidden fear of missing out. The Single-Minded person talks about their strict diet or unwavering loyalty to chocolate mousse, reflecting a decisive, no-nonsense approach. You may see patterns with the reserved state of capacity. The Sampler explains their desire to try a bit of everything without going overboard—balance is key for them. This is where behaviors from a state of maximized capacity are observed. Meanwhile, the Indecisive one sheepishly reveals their struggle with too many choices and a fear of making the wrong one, highlighting their fatigue in the face of decisions—classic behaviors of someone in a fatigued state of capacity.

This dessert-based revelation is not just a fun activity; it's a comedic yet poignant mirror of real-life decision-making. Whether it's choosing a dessert or committing to a new project, our patterns tend to repeat. By reflecting on something as simple as how we choose our treats, we gain insight into our broader decision-making habits. So next time you're at a buffet or facing a big life choice, remember: your dessert plate might just be telling you something important about yourself.

The Dangers of Ego: Alex's Story

Alex, a young professional with boundless ambition and a relentless drive to succeed, was fueled by the belief that busyness was synonymous with success. The more they filled their calendar, the more valuable they felt. Every day was a new opportunity to prove their worth, to show that they could handle anything thrown their way. They were the epitome of hustle culture and proud of it.

But behind the facade of their packed schedule was a creeping exhaustion. Their calendar resembled a chaotic jigsaw puzzle, with pieces that didn't fit—meetings stacked on top of each other, deadlines looming like dark clouds, and social commitments squeezed in as though time could somehow bend to their will. Alex thrived on the chaos, convinced that their ability to juggle it all was proof of their value. However, as the weeks passed, something began to shift. The excitement of the relentless pace started to fade, replaced by a sense of dread each time their phone buzzed with another notification. Despite the outward success, Alex couldn't shake the feeling that they were slipping—losing control, losing joy, losing themself. And yet, they couldn't stop. Ego whispered in their ear, convincing them that saying no, slowing down, or admitting they needed a break would be seen as failure.

As Ryan Holiday emphasizes in *Ego Is the Enemy*, the unchecked ego becomes a saboteur, convincing us that we are only as good as our next achievement. For Alex, the ego was an invisible hand guiding them further into burnout, telling them to push harder, to keep proving themselves, even when it was costing them their well-being. The fear of not being seen as enough kept them in a cycle of overcommitment, leaving them too depleted to enjoy the very success they worked so hard to achieve.

It wasn't until Alex faced a health scare—one that forced them to take a step back—that they realized how destructive the need to prove themself had become. They had built their life around external validation, striving for a capacity net worth that could never be fully satisfied. What started as ambition had morphed into a toxic relationship with work and self-worth. In that moment of clarity, Alex began to deconstruct the layers of their hustle and ambition. They learned, as Holiday describes, that true success isn't about conquering everything, but about mastering the ability to choose what truly matters. It was a humbling realization that allowed Alex to reset, realign, and reframe their approach to life—not through ego, but through intentional and meaningful decisions.

Alex's story reminds us that ego, when unchecked, can sabotage not only our capacity for success, but also our well-being. It's a lesson that resonates with so many who find themselves trapped in the relentless pursuit of more, only to realize they've lost sight of themselves along the way. The pressures of ambition and the silent influence of ego can push us to overextend ourselves, leading to burnout and frustration. Their experience serves as a powerful reminder that unchecked ego, while initially fueling success, can eventually upset the balance we all seek in our lives.

Alex's journey is one that many of us can relate to—pushing ourselves to the brink, thinking that more is always better, only to realize we've lost control of our time, energy, and well-being. The cracks begin to show when we've committed to too much and let our ego convince us that slowing down is not an option. But what if we could unravel that pressure and find clarity?

This is where the Egocake Tool comes in. Just like Alex, we often layer on increasingly, feeling overwhelmed by the choices we've made or the obligations we've taken on. Egocake helps you step back, deconstruct those layers, and identify which commitments are no longer serving you. It gives you the space to resign from the relentless pursuit of "more" and choose, with intention, what truly deserves your focus and energy.

If you've ever found yourself in Alex's predicament—juggling too much, feeling burned out, and wondering how to regain balance—the Egocake Tool is designed to help you regain control. It offers a simple yet powerful way to evaluate where you are now and what needs to shift in order for you to feel more aligned with your values and capacity. By peeling back the layers of unnecessary distractions and obligations, you can make better decisions for yourself moving forward. Let's dive into how you can start applying this tool today.

The Lesson: Ego and You

Picture this: you're managing a small team at work, and everyone is feeling overwhelmed by an extensive list of tasks. Deadlines are looming, and it's starting to feel like you're not making meaningful progress. Instead of throwing more energy at the problem, you introduce Egocake. As a team, you sit down and break everything down layer by layer—what's necessary, what's just noise, and what's causing burnout. After the exercise, the team is more focused. You've resigned from the unnecessary commitments, and everyone has a clearer sense of what truly deserves their attention. The difference? Less stress, better productivity, and more energy to give to the projects that matter.

Or imagine a more individual scenario. You've got a to-do list that never ends. You're juggling work, family, social obligations, and self-care, but it feels like there's never enough time. With Egocake, you take a step back and peel away the layers of distraction and overcommitment. Maybe you realize that volunteering for every work event isn't aligning with your long-term goals, or that you're saying yes out of obligation rather than true interest. By trimming off those unnecessary tasks, you free up time and energy for what truly resonates with you—whether that's spending time with family, focusing on personal growth, or knocking out that big project at work.

Egocake doesn't just help you get more done—it makes your efforts *count*. You'll notice a boost in productivity, but more importantly you'll be working with a clearer purpose. That overwhelming feeling? It starts to fade because you're making mindful choices, aligned with your values and capacity, not just your available hours.

The tool is also a game-changer for team dynamics. Picture a team that's not just busy but engaged, focused on tasks that align with both the team's goals and each member's strengths. The energy shift is immediate—less burnout, more motivation, and better outcomes because everyone's on the same page about what's worth their time.

Whether you're leading a team or managing your personal commitments, Egocake helps you cut through the chaos and focus on what truly matters—without stretching yourself too thin and snapping.

Chapter Twelve

Capacity Elasticity—Create Sustainable Capacity without It Snapping

If everything is important, nothing is important. — Patrick Lencioni

Diary Entry

*T*his is my breaking point.

I did it again! Hit burnout. It wasn't a sudden realization but a gradual decline, evident in the malfunctioning of my executive functions. My mind couldn't perform quick math calculations, and simple questions from my kids left me stuttering, trying to jolt my brain into action. Yet amidst these glaring signs, I pushed forward with the mantra I CAN MANAGE!

Ignoring the flashing warning signs became my norm until stress and fatigue manifested physically as a painful condition called frozen shoulder. Juggling multiple responsibilities—teaching, parenting, growing my business, and supporting my husband through his studies and work as an elementary school principal—became unbearable.

The pivotal question arose: what could I resign from? The answer didn't come easy for someone accustomed to high-capacity multitasking. Eventually, I made the difficult decision to reduce my workload and income by cutting back my hours at the college.

The emotions that followed were a cocktail of shame, guilt, and fear of judgment, compounded by the impact on my lifestyle and finances. Approaching HR felt like a further blow when they confessed they hadn't handled such a request in years, their confusion and lack of support only deepening my sense of isolation. I stood there, realizing that the very system I had relied on was unprepared to help, leaving me to navigate the situation alone. The shock of this revelation was a harsh reminder of how far I had fallen, and the disappointment in myself was almost unbearable. My shame grew as I confronted the stark reality that I had overextended myself to the point where even seeking help felt like another failure.

Are You a Victim or Inflictor of Capacity Creep?

Have you ever found yourself stretched beyond your limits, "borrowing" capacity from others without even realizing it? This phenomenon is known as capacity creep—encroaching on someone else's time, energy, and resources. It might be a spouse, a colleague, or a friend.

You know that feeling when you're so eager to help that the word *yes* slips out before your brain can catch up? Yeah, that's me. I've developed a bit of a habit of saying yes to just about everything—whether it's organizing events, lending a hand with a project, or even baking cupcakes for a charity drive that needed them ... *yesterday*. And then, somewhere between commitment #72 and #73, it dawns on me: I'm stretched so thin that I've basically become human taffy.

But here's where the real magic of capacity creep happens. Instead of recognizing my own limits and saying no, I have a secret weapon. Enter my husband, Chris. In moments of peak overcommitment, I've become an expert in volunteering him to take over. Family BBQ needs someone to mind the grill? "Chris will do it!" Need someone to help move heavy furniture? "Chris will do it!" It's reached a point where our circle of family and friends knows the routine—if I'm in over my head, Chris is about to get recruited. It's like the unspoken rule: when I run out of steam, Chris steps in (whether he's aware of it or not)!

The Season of September

As summer winds down, many of us start winding up: signing up for new activities, enrolling kids in programs, setting new goals for the fall, and revising budgets after a YOLO summer. New fitness and health regimes often come into play, and before you know it, your to-do list is never-ending. By the time September rolls around, you may find yourself overcommitted. This can lead to you asking others to manage tasks you would normally do yourself, or even "voluntelling" people around you. We all know that's not fair or respectful. Overcommitment is a part of being human. However, respecting your capacity—and that of others—is also crucial. It's a responsible form of self-care.

Before diving into the upcoming season, step away from your busy calendar. Take a moment to consider what a capacity-respecting and capacity-honoring schedule looks like. This reflection can help you manage your commitments better and avoid the pitfalls of capacity creep. Many clients push back at this recommendation and tell me they have to operate like this because everything needs to get done. In the same breath, they often express that they just don't have the time to do the things they love. I gently *also* push back to let them know they do have time, but their capacity is being eroded somewhere. We just need to figure out where, so we can focus on the most important tasks.

So, as you plan for the months ahead, remember to prioritize what truly matters. Identify where your capacity is being drained and make adjustments to ensure you're honoring your commitments without overwhelming yourself or those around you. This approach will help you maintain a healthier balance and enjoy more of the things you love.

The Stretch and Snap: Understanding Capacity Elasticity

Capacity Elasticity® is a powerful concept designed to visually demonstrate the limits of our capacity and the dangers of overextending ourselves. Imagine a rubber band—when you stretch it, it can accommodate more, just as we can take on additional tasks, commitments, and responsibilities. However, as the rubber band stretches, it becomes increasingly taut, signaling that it's nearing its breaking point. This is precisely what happens when we continuously push beyond our natural limits. In the short term, it might seem manageable, but over time, the tension builds, and without proper management, the band—our capacity—will eventually snap. Envision your own capacity as that rubber band. Reflect on how far you've stretched it and consider whether you're close to that critical point. The key is to recognize when you need to release some tension, allowing the band to return to its natural state. This awareness is crucial for maintaining balance and avoiding the burnout that comes from living in a state of constant overstretch.

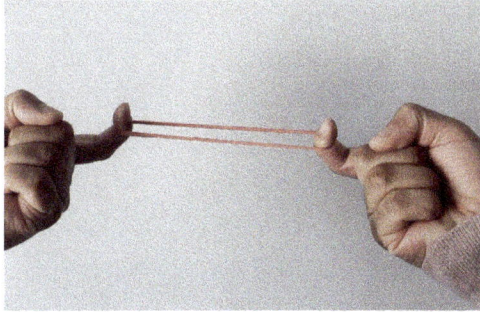

One of the Biggest and Most Untapped Competitive Advantages

Human capacity is one of our biggest competitive advantages, yet mental health concerns and mental health days, as well as burnout rates, are all on the rise. And yet we see so many companies spending billions of dollars to engage their employees more! We need to redirect our energy and dollars. I don't think we should be throwing money at engaging people more; many are already engaged and ready to work. What we need is to work more closely and collaboratively at leveraging and caring for people's capacity more.

One of most basic and simple thoughts I've ever received from a coach of mine that has had the longest-lasting impact was this: "Mel, every time you say yes to something, you are saying no to something else." (A line he might of read in one of Ryan Holiday's books.)

Let that sink in.

Sadly, in my own case, I was saying yes to work but no to my family and friends. The people I loved the most were the last pick in my lineup of life choices. How could this be?

The irony is that many people decide to leave their full-time jobs and start their own, thinking and believing they are creating a better life for themselves and their family. They romanticize the five-hour workweek, work-life balance, the seven-figure paychecks, the vacations, the being your own boss. What they don't realize is that starting a business requires more hours than high-achieving corporate people do every week. Your business becomes part of your family, something you have to raise, nourish, care for, and hire people to work for it while it grows. Its success is contingent on your level of care and dedication.

This is what I did. I left corporate, started teaching, and started a business. Early on, my accountant sat me down and told me, "Something is not measuring up: your expenditures are bigger than your profits." I was completely defensive: how dare he criticize my spending habits, my "investments" in my business! In reality, he wasn't concerned with how much I was earning or losing; he was simply highlighting that my business wasn't generating any profit. The truth was, I had been treating my business more like a hobby, hesitant to step back and face the possibility of exceeding my own expectations. Stretching my capacity and confidence responsibly was essential, but it demanded significant leaps of faith.

In *The Big Leap*, Gay Hendricks discusses the concept of the "Upper Limit Problem," which refers to the self-imposed barriers that prevent us from achieving our full potential. These barriers often manifest as feelings of unworthiness, fear of success, or subconscious behaviors that sabotage our progress when we start to experience increased levels of success, happiness, or fulfillment. Hendricks suggests that these limitations are ingrained from childhood and form a ceiling within our comfort zones.

When we approach this upper limit, our fear of going all in and breaking through can trigger self-sabotaging actions, like procrastination, unnecessary distractions, or even creating crises that prevent us from succeeding. This self-sabotage is a way our subconscious mind tries to keep us within the safe bounds of our comfort zones, thereby preventing the discomfort that comes with stretching beyond our perceived limits. To overcome this, Hendricks advises recognizing and becoming aware of these self-sabotaging patterns. By consciously identifying when we hit these upper limits, we can start to address and dissolve them, allowing us to stretch ourselves just enough to break through and achieve higher levels of success and fulfillment.

It took me three burnouts to understand that opportunity can stretch me to an unrealistic breaking point. There are five key questions that help me in this situation:

1. My time — Do I have the time for this commitment or is my calendar booked?

2. My ability — Do I have the skills to successfully complete this or will I have to learn something new?

3. My money — Do I have the financial resources to commit to this or will I incur debt?

4. My passion — Is this commitment aligned with my purpose and will it bring me joy?

5. My season — Is this the right season for this commitment?

Saying no isn't easy, but as we discussed in chapters 7 and 10 there are gracious and respectful ways to politely decline. Instead of saying, "I just don't have the time," I now say, "I just don't have the capacity for that right now."

Boundary setting is crucial in maintaining a balanced life, allowing us to safeguard our time, energy, and mental well-being. However, even with strong boundaries, we often find ourselves grappling with irresistible habits that undermine our efforts. These habits, deeply ingrained in our daily routines, can quietly erode the very boundaries we've set. Transitioning from boundary setting to fixing irresistible habits requires us to identify these behaviors, understand their triggers, and implement strategies to reshape them. By addressing these habits, we can strengthen our boundaries and create a more sustainable, healthy lifestyle.

Understanding and Fixing Irresistible Habits

In *Atomic Habits*, James Clear delves into the mechanics of habits, offering insights into why certain behaviors become irresistible and how to address the underlying causes to develop healthier habits. Clear outlines a framework that helps individuals understand the cues and rewards that drive their habits and provides practical strategies for making lasting changes.

Here is the approach to habit formation based on his "Four Laws of Behavior Change: Make It Obvious, Make It Attractive, Make It Easy, and Make It Satisfying." To break irresistible habits, it's essential to understand and invert these laws.

1. **Make It Invisible:** Break an irresistible habit by reducing exposure to the cues that trigger it. For example, if social media are a distraction, you might remove the app from your phone or use website blockers to limit access. By making the cue invisible, you reduce the temptation.

2. **Make It Unattractive:** Reprogram your mind to see the negative aspects of the habit. This involves reframing your thoughts about the habit to highlight its downsides. For instance, you might remind yourself of the time wasted on unproductive activities or the negative impact on your well-being. By making the habit unattractive, you decrease its appeal.

3. **Make It Difficult:** Increase the friction associated with the habit so as to help break it. This might mean changing your environment to make the habit harder to perform. If you want to stop snacking on unhealthy food, you could store it in hard-to-reach places or avoid buying it altogether. By making the habit difficult, you reduce the likelihood of engaging in it.

4. **Make It Unsatisfying:** Make it unsatisfying (it bears repeating!). This can be achieved by creating immediate negative consequences for the behavior. For example, you could implement a penalty for every time you indulge in the habit, such as donating to a cause you dislike. Additionally, involving an accountability partner can add social pressure and make the habit less satisfying.

The Role of Identity in Habit Change

James Clear highlights how important identity is in building lasting habits. Instead of focusing only on the end goal, like losing weight or saving money, Clear suggests thinking about the kind of person you want to become. For example, instead of just aiming to lose weight, start seeing yourself as someone who prioritizes health. This mindset shift makes your habits feel more natural and sustainable because they become part of who you are, not just what you do.

To get started, keep it simple. Focus on creating small, manageable habits that you can stick to easily, like taking the stairs or drinking more water. As these little habits become part of your routine, you can gradually build on them. This approach helps you make progress without getting overwhelmed, and as your confidence grows, so does your ability to take on bigger challenges. Bit by bit, you're becoming the person you want to be.

Dr. Benjamin Hardy takes a similar idea but digs deeper into how we can shape our future selves. According to Hardy, the first step is having a clear idea of who you want to become and setting specific, meaningful goals that match that vision. But it's not just about setting goals—it's about deeply committing to them and taking ownership of your progress. Hardy talks about the importance of creating an environment that supports your growth, whether that means surrounding yourself with positive influences or setting up routines that keep you on track.

Hardy also encourages stepping out of your comfort zone. The idea is to take bold actions that move you toward the future you've envisioned, even if they feel a bit scary. And just as importantly, he emphasizes regularly reflecting on your progress, being open to feedback, and adjusting your course as needed. The goal is to stay aligned with the person you want to become, learning from your experiences along the way.

Both Clear and Hardy offer down-to-earth advice for anyone looking to create lasting change. Clear focuses on the small, consistent habits that gradually shape who you are, while Hardy encourages a more intentional commitment to your future self. Together, they show how a combination of simple habits and big-picture thinking can help you grow into the person you genuinely want to be.

Chapter Thirteen

Redefining the Boundaries: Teaching Others to Honor Your Capacity

You are always teaching people how to treat you. — Melanie Sodka

Diary Entry

*C*heers to you!

Yes, you.

The one with a thousand commitments.

The one who almost never says no.

The one who has great intentions but no capacity to fulfill them.

The one who everyone else expects to say yes to every request.

The one who wants to please and make people happy (and yet feels guilty for it).

Every. Single. Time.

When you are ready to finally say no, your inner core rumbles and convinces you to say yes. One. Last. Time.

And when you do finally say the dirty little word—psst, it's no btw—people treat you differently.

But … it gets easier. Every time that powerful two-letter word trickles out of your mouth. I promise.

How?

BECAUSE YOU TEACH PEOPLE HOW TO TREAT YOU.

So teach them that you DO NOT have superpowers. (Sorry to burst the bubble of all of your admirers.)

That saying yes will tip your capacity. It will force you to sacrifice time elsewhere. Time that should be non-negotiable.

You got this.

So, cheers to you and your precious capacity.

Recognizing Sustainable Success: The Impact and Purpose of the Healthy Hustle Awards

As mentioned in chapter 8, the Healthy Hustle Awards, created to counter the glorification of overwork, proved to be a transformative initiative. First implemented with a client, the awards highlighted accountability and gathered authentic stories, showing that prioritizing well-being did not diminish productivity. The positive feedback from employees, who experienced enhanced performance through better self-care, reinforced the value of investing in a balanced work-life approach. This initiative demonstrated that fostering a healthy work culture leads to sustainable success, benefiting both individuals and organizations.

The success of the Healthy Hustle Awards also underscored a crucial lesson: we are always training people how to treat us. By setting boundaries and valuing our own health and time, we signal to others the importance of respect and balance. This concept is pivotal in both personal and professional settings, influencing how we are perceived and treated. In the following examples, we'll explore how implementing these principles can reshape interactions, fostering environments that honor well-being and productivity. Here are a few success stories.

Success Stories with Capacity Management Tools

Story 1: Clara's Journey to Work-Life Balance

Background: Clara, a marketing executive, was overwhelmed by her workload and constant notifications from work and social media. She often found herself staying late at the office, missing family dinners, and feeling perpetually exhausted.

Problem: Despite trying various quick fixes like meditation apps, stress-relief supplements, and online therapy subscriptions, Clara's stress levels remained high. These solutions provided temporary relief but didn't address the root cause of her burnout.

Capacity Management Tool: Clara decided to use the Capacity Creator's CHIEFF of Your Capacity tool, which helps individuals allocate time and evaluate the quality of their capacity in Career, Health, Intellectual, Emotional, Financial, Fun, Spirituality, and Family categories.

Implementation:

1. **Assessment:** Clara used the CHIEFF system to evaluate her current capacity. She realized that her Career and Health lights were red, while Family and Fun were yellow, and the rest were green.

2. **Reallocation:** She reallocated her time, dedicating specific hours to work, health (morning jogs), and family (weekend activities). She also set boundaries for work-related notifications.

3. **Commitment:** Clara committed to her new schedule and used weekly check-ins to adjust and stay on track.

Results:

- **Long-Term Effectiveness:** Within a few months, Clara noticed a significant improvement in her work-life balance. Her Career and Health lights turned green, indicating reduced stress and better overall well-being.

- **Sustainable Changes:** Unlike the short-term fixes, the capacity management tool helped Clara create a sustainable routine that she could maintain without extra costs.

Story 2: Jayden's Path to Financial Stability and Mental Peace

Background: Jayden, a small business owner, was constantly stressed about his finances. He tried various short-term solutions like financial planning apps and stress-relief gadgets, but his anxiety about money persisted.

Problem: These short-term solutions didn't provide a comprehensive understanding of his financial situation or help him develop a clear strategy for long-term stability.

Capacity Management Tool: Jayden turned to the 3x3 capacity matrix to organize his roles, goals, and controls.

Implementation:

1. **Roles and Goals:** Jayden used the 3x3 method: Business Owner, Father, and Personal Finance Manager. For each role, he set clear goals. For example, under Personal Finance Manager, his goal was to create a sustainable budget and build an emergency fund.

2. **Controls:** He established controls by tracking his expenses and income, setting monthly financial reviews, and celebrating small milestones like saving a specific amount.

3. **Action Plan:** Jayden broke down his goals into actionable steps, such as reducing unnecessary expenses, increasing business revenue, and setting aside savings regularly.

Results:

- **Long-Term Effectiveness:** Over time, Jayden achieved financial stability and peace of mind. His emergency fund grew, and he developed a healthier relationship with money.

- **Sustainable Changes:** The capacity management tool provided Jayden with a clear framework to manage his finances without relying on expensive apps or services. The changes were integrated into his daily life, making them sustainable and effective.

Story 3: Mila's Emotional and Intellectual Growth

Background: Mila, a teacher, felt emotionally drained and intellectually unstimulated. She tried various short-term solutions like self-help books and online courses, but they didn't provide lasting fulfillment.

Problem: These solutions were often generic and didn't cater to her specific needs, leading to short-lived motivation and recurring feelings of inadequacy.

Capacity Management Tools: Mila decided to use the Value Mining and the Art of Resignment exercises along with the Capacity Creator framework to realign her life with her core values and goals.

Implementation:

1. **Value Mining: Mila** identified her top three values: Connection, Growth, and Contribution. She recognized that her current routine didn't align well with these values.

2. **Re-evaluation and Resignment:** She reassessed her commitments and decided to resign from activities that didn't serve her values. For example, she stepped back from an extra committee at work that wasn't fulfilling.

3. **New Commitments:** Mila committed to activities that aligned with her values, such as joining a local book club (Growth), volunteering (Contribution), and spending more quality time with friends and family (Connection).

Results:

- **Long-Term Effectiveness:** Fatima experienced a renewed sense of purpose and energy. Her emotional well-being improved, and she felt intellectually stimulated by her new activities.

- **Sustainable Changes:** By focusing on her core values, Mila integrated meaningful changes into her daily life. These changes didn't require ongoing purchases or subscriptions, making them both cost-effective and enduring.

Unlocking Your Capacity: Measuring Productivity, Balance, and Sustainable Success

After witnessing the transformative power of capacity management tools, it's undeniable that optimizing your capacity leads to real, measurable benefits—enhanced productivity, reduced stress, and a stronger sense of balance. These tools empower you to pinpoint where your time and energy are being spent and help you align your efforts with your core values and goals. As you reflect on your journey and the progress you've made, I challenge you to consider two important questions:

1. Are you operating in a capacity overdraft, consistently pushing beyond your limits?

2. What is your capacity net worth—the true measure of your sustainable productivity and well-being?

These questions are designed to provoke thought and guide you toward a more balanced and fulfilling approach to managing your capacity.

Let's dive deeper into these concepts. As mentioned, capacity has elasticity—much like a bank account, your capacity has a limit. This limit, akin to a financial overdraft, is the point where there is simply nothing left to give. Yet, many of us flirt with this limit, stretching ourselves just to get through to the next "payday." This cycle, if unchecked, leads to burnout. We tell ourselves that an extra hour of sleep, an extra cup of coffee, or another round of pills will get us through. Or that a good cry or an outburst will provide the release we need to keep going. But living with these crutches—these "ifs," "whens," and "hopefullys"—is not sustainable. Just as for substance abuse, abusing our capacity is an addiction to the next "hit." We must ask ourselves: what are we really doing?

Now consider your capacity net worth. Just as you manage your finances, you should also manage your capacity with care. Your capacity net worth is the value of your network and tribe, minus the debt of those who don't truly support you. Your investment is the consistent value you offer to your clients and community. Your debt represents the people and choices that drain you—those who don't contribute positively to your growth. Your return on investment reflects the loyalty and support of those who stand by you because you serve them well.

So let's put this into perspective. If your supporters are genuinely invested in you, wouldn't your ROI increase substantially? What about your investments—are you consistently contributing value that creates compound interest in your relationships and impact? Are you truly growing your influence and reach? And crucially, what would your community look like if you removed the "bought" people or those who don't genuinely care about you or your work? Would your net worth drop, or would it actually reflect a more authentic, sustainable capacity? These questions are designed to challenge you, encouraging you to rethink how you manage your capacity and how you measure true success in your life and work.

The Value of Community

I once added up all the communities I belonged to, including Facebook groups, paid communities, volunteer groups, committees, and other affiliations. I belonged to sixteen communities, big and small, but nonetheless this was outrageous and unsustainable. How could I possibly be a quality contributor to so many? Consider this: there are twenty-four hours in a day, and assuming an average of eight hours of sleep, we are left with sixteen waking hours. Out of these, many of us spend around eight hours working, leaving us with another eight hours for other activities. If each community required an average of two hours per week, that's thirty-two hours a week just for community commitments—almost five hours a day. This calculation doesn't even account for personal responsibilities, leisure, or self-care.

One by one, I went through each of my commitments, aligning each with my values. It became clear that some communities were easy to join but difficult to contribute to meaningfully. The ones in which I had overindulged were draining my capacity without offering significant returns in fulfillment or value alignment. It was evident I needed to resign from some and reallocate my efforts to others. By reducing my commitments and focusing on the communities that truly mattered to me, I was able to contribute more effectively and enhance the quality of my participation. This process not only alleviated my overwhelm but also allowed me to invest my time and energy where it would have the most impact, both for myself and for the communities I chose to stay committed to.

Capacity management tools like CHIEFF, the 3x3 capacity matrix, and the Value Mining exercise provide individuals with practical and sustainable strategies to manage their lives effectively. These tools address the root causes of stress and imbalance, leading to long-lasting results without the high price tags associated with short-term solutions. By integrating these strategies into everyday life, individuals can achieve meaningful and enduring improvements in their well-being.

Chapter Fourteen

Invest in Health or Pay the Price: The Time Trade-off

If you don't make time for exercise, you will probably have to make time for illness. — Robin Sharma

Diary Entry

*I*t's like an old injury that keeps coming back.

It's like an addiction you are always recovering from.

Its associated behaviors are not easily eradicated.

Eventually you end up adopting burnout behaviors and habits that provide the temporary surge capacity needed in the clutch or the eleventh hour.

But soon the eleventh hour becomes an hour and you simply don't have any more hours.

You find yourself benched because you are running a deficit (again), and the repercussions keep getting worse each time.

Boundaries, Burnout, and EAPs

I used to sprain my ankle while playing basketball. *Repeatedly*, until I finally wore a brace. The brace gave me boundaries. The doctor allowed me to discover my range of motion. Gave me physiotherapy exercises to strengthen it. I now know that playing sports without a brace will increase my risk of reinjury. And I used to sprain my brain into burnout. *Also* repeatedly, until I installed boundaries. The therapist allowed me to discover my mental range of motion, my weak spots, my guilty pleasures, and indulgences, and my "watch-out" behaviors for becoming a repeat offender. The therapist also gave me exercises to work on to strengthen my mental and emotional capacity. I now know that my high propensity for work can injure my brain again. My personality style and emotional intelligence create a perfect combination for addiction, low self-control, and impulsive decision-making. Understanding the state of capacity, we are most driven to based on our current circumstances and predisposal to certain tendencies is essential to preserving a healthy mindset and avoiding burnout. Just as I relied on a therapist to help me build boundaries and strengthen my mental capacity, Employee Assistance Programs (EAPs) can be a valuable resource for employees facing similar challenges. However, the reality behind EAPs is more complex than it appears.

Employee Assistance Programs (EAPs) are widely implemented in workplaces, but their effectiveness varies. While most companies offer these programs, I've observed that many employees hesitate to take advantage of them, even when the support is readily available. From my experience, there's often a disconnect between knowing these resources exist and feeling comfortable enough to use them. This hesitation can stem from several factors, including lack of awareness, concerns about confidentiality, and the stigma surrounding mental health support. As a result, EAPs remain underutilized, despite their potential to provide meaningful help.

Even when employees do use EAPs, the outcomes are not always successful. While some studies report high satisfaction and clinical improvements among users, other data indicates significant gaps. For instance, forty-two percent of employees who need therapy are rejected, and there is a general dissatisfaction with the services provided. Furthermore, fifty-five percent of workers believe that their employer overestimates the mental health support provided by the workplace environment, and many employees remain underserved due to the inadequate promotion and visibility of EAP services. (See Hanisch et al., Mental Health America, and Hylant.)

Research suggests that EAPs are often less effective because they are not fully integrated into the overall mental health strategy of the organization. They may be seen as a standalone solution rather than part of a broader, proactive approach to employee well-being. Overall, while EAPs have the potential to offer significant benefits, their success depends on proper implementation, promotion, and integration into a comprehensive mental health strategy. Employers need to address these challenges to enhance the effectiveness and utilization of EAPs. (See Attridge and World Health Organization.)

In Canada, coverage for mental health services through insurance plans varies widely. Most Canadians with employer-based or private health benefits have access to some form of mental health coverage, but the extent of that coverage differs. Typically, insurance plans offer between $500 and $12,500 annually for mental health services, with some covering a percentage of each session's cost (ranging from 25% to 100%) or a limited number of sessions per year. Despite this, many Canadians face barriers, such as out-of-pocket costs and limited sessions, which can prevent them from accessing the care they need. (Informed Choices, Sana Counselling, CIHI)

On average, the cost for a counseling session with a registered psychotherapist in Canada ranges from $90 to $170, while sessions with psychologists can be higher, typically between $200 and $500 per session. Many workplace insurance plans offer coverage for mental health services, but the extent of coverage can vary significantly. Some plans may cover a set number of sessions (e.g., ten to fifteen sessions annually) or provide a specific dollar amount towards counseling services.(Sana Counselling, Therapy Alberta, First Session)

Most People Choose Suffering over Surrendering

Ryan Holiday writes in *Ego Is the Enemy* that "if your purpose is something larger than you—if it's to accomplish something, to prove something to yourself—then suddenly everything becomes both easier and more difficult." I became curious about surrendering and suffering and wanted to explore more. The juxtaposition of surrender and suffering highlights the contrast between a state of peace and acceptance versus a state of resistance and pain. The following were relationships I explored in order to expand my capacity while accessing my true sense of self.

1. **Control vs Letting Go:** While suffering is often tied to the need for control and the frustration when things don't go as planned, surrender is about letting go of that control and finding peace in the uncertainty. We all need a sense of control at times to feel safe, however some of us experience this polarizing behavior more frequently and intensely

than others do. As discussed in chapter 4, there are specific personality styles that are more rigid in their behaviors. But the practice of letting go and learning how to surrender to circumstances out of your control will almost always bring you peace and reduce stress.

2. **Resistance vs Acceptance:** Suffering is marked by resistance to what is, while surrender is marked by acceptance. This acceptance does not mean passivity but rather a proactive embrace of the present.

3. **Fear vs Trust:** Suffering is fueled by fear—fear of the unknown, fear of loss, fear of pain. Surrender, however, is grounded in trust—trust in oneself, in others, and in the larger unfolding of life. I lived in the fear of loss. I was programmed that way from the unprocessed grief, and it became the operating system in decision-making. When insecurity crept in, my fear would take the wheel and drive the bus. My subconscious was wired from an early age to fear losing a person, a relationship, and/or an opportunity. My overcommitment tendencies can be mapped to this fear and I'm still working on recognizing it when it shows up. Trusting myself has always been a battle even though my intuition is inexplicably strong. My husband calls me a witch because of my strong intuitive nature that can produce premonitions.

4. **Stagnation vs Flow:** Suffering can lead to stagnation, where an individual feels stuck in their pain. Surrender, conversely, allows for flow and movement, enabling growth and transformation. Once I started to heal, took the medication, had the hard conversations, freed myself from unrealistic beliefs, and gave myself space, I was able to access a flow state where ideas would flood my soul, when my true authentic self could come out and play. Overwhelm and too many options lead to stagnation. When we are burdened and bogged down, we can't get into a flow state and access true happiness and stillness. Think of water. If water doesn't move and sits for too long, it stagnates, unlike a river, which winds its way through the rocks and edges, flowing and ultimately reaching its destination, the ocean.

5. **Isolation vs Connection:** Suffering often isolates, creating a sense

of being alone in your pain. Surrender, on the other hand, fosters connection, as it opens you up to the support and empathy of others. Isolation can lead to mental health issues, exacerbating feelings of loneliness, anxiety, and depression. As humans, we are wired for connection. Developing relationships and creating bonds are integral to our well-being. It's something that nourishes us, providing a sense of belonging, purpose, and emotional resilience. By surrendering the need to carry burdens alone, we allow ourselves to experience the healing power of community and shared humanity.

Understanding the delicate balance between surrendering and suffering is crucial in our journey toward well-being. Surrendering involves letting go of control and accepting our limitations, while suffering often stems from resisting this acceptance.

When the Body Says No

Gabor Maté's book, *When the Body Says No*, delves into the profound connection between the mind and body, illustrating how stress and suppressed emotions manifest as physical ailments. This theme can be used to amplify and support the experiences of burnout you've had in your twenties, thirties, and forties, recognizing how your body has been communicating distress throughout these periods.

Twenties: The Initial Signs of Burnout

In your twenties, like many high achievers, you likely pushed yourself hard, driven by ambition and a desire to prove yourself. According to Maté, the body begins to signal distress when the mind is under chronic stress. You might have experienced frequent headaches, gastrointestinal issues, or frequent colds and flus—early warning signs that your body was struggling to cope with the relentless pace you were maintaining. Maté explains that the suppression of emotions, particularly the constant need to meet external expectations and the fear of disappointing others, can lead to these initial physical manifestations.

Thirties: The Escalation of Symptoms

Entering your thirties, the stress likely intensified as personal and professional responsibilities grew. Maté describes how chronic stress and emotional repression can escalate to more severe health issues if the underlying causes are not addressed. In this decade, you might have noticed more significant health problems such as insomnia, anxiety, or even more serious autoimmune conditions. These symptoms were your body's way of saying no, urging you to address the deep-seated emotional issues and the unsustainable demands you were placing on yourself.

Forties: The Critical Phase

By your forties, the cumulative effect of years of stress and emotional repression likely resulted in more severe burnout. Maté highlights that prolonged exposure to stress hormones can lead to chronic illnesses such as hypertension, heart disease, or severe mental health issues like depression. This decade might have been a critical phase where your body demanded urgent attention, making it clear that continuing on the same path was no longer viable. The body's louder, more alarming signals were an unequivocal plea for you to reevaluate your lifestyle, emotional health, and boundaries.

Gabor Maté's work emphasizes that our bodies are constantly communicating with us, often through symptoms that we might dismiss as minor inconveniences. These physical manifestations are crucial messages that reflect our emotional and psychological state. Understanding and acknowledging these messages involve:

- Noticing recurring symptoms and their correlation with periods of high stress or emotional turmoil.

- Becoming more aware of your emotional state and how it affects your physical health, including acknowledging feelings of overwhelm, anxiety, and the pressure of meeting others' expectations.

- Learning to say no and resign from commitments that no longer serve your well-being.

- Practicing self-compassion and giving yourself permission to rest and recover without guilt.

By drawing on Maté's insights, you can frame your experiences of burnout as a narrative of your body's persistent efforts to communicate the need for change. This understanding can foster a more compassionate and initiative-taking approach to managing your health and well-being, honoring your body's messages and prioritizing self-care. Recognizing burnout as your body's way of signaling the need for change is just the first step in managing it effectively. While understanding these signals is crucial, it's equally important to know how to respond to them in a way that completes the process of stress relief. This is where the concept of the stress cycle becomes invaluable. By addressing not just the sources of stress, but also how our bodies hold onto it, we can begin to take actionable steps toward recovery. The stress cycle provides a framework for doing just that—helping us physically process and release the stress that accumulates, even after the stressors themselves have passed.

The Stress Cycle

In their book, *Burnout: The Secret to Unlocking the Stress Cycle*, Emily Nagoski and Amelia Nagoski discuss the crucial role of completing the stress cycle in managing burnout. They explain that stress is a physical reaction that must be dealt with physically. Simply removing the stressor, such as finishing a project or resolving a conflict, does not necessarily remove the stress from the body. The authors emphasize that to truly alleviate stress, one must complete the stress cycle, which can involve various physical activities and emotional expressions.

- **Physical Activity:** Engaging in exercise, even as simple as a twenty-minute walk, helps to metabolize stress hormones and restore the body's equilibrium.

- **Breathing:** Deep, slow breaths can signal the parasympathetic nervous system to calm the body down.

- **Positive Social Interaction:** Brief, friendly interactions can reinforce a sense of connection and safety.

- **Laughter:** Genuine laughter can reduce stress and improve emotional well-being.

- **Affection:** Physical affection, such as a hug that lasts at least twenty seconds, can release oxytocin and lower stress levels.

- **Crying:** Allowing oneself to cry can be a powerful way to release pent-up emotions.

- **Creative Expression:** Activities such as painting, writing, or playing music can help process and release stress.

The Nagoski sisters underscore that these methods are not one-size-fits-all, and individuals should find what works best for them. By incorporating these practices into daily life, one can more effectively manage stress and prevent burnout.

The Burnout Prevention Method™

Imagine your life is like a favorite song. The rhythm and beats per minute (BPM) dictate the energy and flow, keeping everything in harmony. Now, think of your daily routine and tasks as the notes in that song. When the BPM is too fast, the song becomes chaotic, and you struggle to keep up with the frantic pace. Conversely, when the BPM is too slow, the song loses its vibrancy and purpose.

This is where *our* BPM—Burnout Prevention Method—comes in. Just like a DJ who perfectly mixes tracks to maintain the right BPM for an unforgettable experience, our program helps you find and maintain the perfect rhythm in your life. We ensure you don't miss a beat by managing your workload, commitments, and personal time.

Our Burnout Prevention Method helps you fine-tune your life's BPM, so you can:

- **Set the Right Tempo:** Identify and prioritize tasks, ensuring you're not overwhelmed by an unmanageable workload.

- **Stay in Sync:** Create a balanced routine that harmonizes work, personal time, and self-care, preventing burnout.

- **Hit the High Notes:** Focus on high-impact activities that align with your values and goals, allowing you to perform at your best without compromising your well-being.

- **Avoid the Dissonance:** Recognize and resign from commitments that no longer serve you, like removing off-beat notes from a song to enhance its melody.

With our BPM, your life can become a symphony of productivity, balance, and fulfillment. Just like a well-composed song that keeps listeners engaged and energized, our method ensures you maintain a sustainable and enjoyable pace, avoiding the burnout that comes from a relentless, unbalanced rhythm.

Prioritizing well-being is not merely a personal choice but a professional and societal necessity. We've seen how neglecting health can lead to profound consequences, both seen and unseen, affecting every aspect of our lives. From diminished productivity to the erosion of mental and emotional resilience, the costs of ignoring our health are far-reaching and significant. Investing in our health, therefore, becomes an investment in our future, our success, and our ability to contribute meaningfully to our communities and organizations.

Chapter Fifteen

Embracing Capacity: Finding Strength in Limits

Within each of us lies an untapped reservoir of potential, waiting to be discovered and celebrated. The beauty in our capacity is not just in what we can achieve, but in how we honor our true selves along the journey. — Melanie Sodka

Final Chapter

I n this final chapter of the book, we delve into the remarkable potential that lies within each of us, celebrating our innate abilities, the strength in our resilience, and the transformative power of embracing our full capacity. It's an invitation to recognize and honor the vast reservoir of talents, skills, and passions that define who we are. We explore how tapping into our true capacity allows us to break free from the constraints of burnout and overwhelm, leading to a more balanced, fulfilling, and impactful life. By understanding and nurturing our capacity, we can achieve a state of flow where our work becomes an expression of our deepest values and aspirations. We also discover practical strategies and inspiring stories that highlight the beauty of living within our capacity, and we learn how to set boundaries that protect our energy, make decisions that align with our purpose, and cultivate habits that support our well-being. As we embrace the full spectrum of our capabilities, we unlock the potential to live more authentically and thrive in every aspect of our lives.

Capacity Bliss: A Transition Out of the State of Indulgence

The sun. The peace. The serenity.

I gave in to the temptation to sit in peace, just for a moment. It felt so good. And I realized that I don't do it enough. Practice serenity, that is.

For a long time, indulgence has been my state of capacity. *Over-indulgence*, actually. I've been trying to get it all done, taking on more just because I thought I could. Running on adrenaline and coffee, and then more coffee. I became addicted to the thrill of squeezing another commitment in. "I can make it work," says the little superhero with the big voice that sits on my shoulder.

But when burnout knocked on my door, I realized many unhealthy habits had gripped my commitments. I had a horrible relationship with time. I was almost always late. Even when I would text in advance to let the person know I was running late, I was reminded that this still qualified as being late. I would schedule events back-to-back with little travel time built in, always saying, "Of course I will be there! Wouldn't miss it for the world!"—even though I wasn't enjoying myself and it probably showed, which wasn't fair to anyone. I relied on my husband to help fulfill my commitments, asking him to get my stuff done so I could uphold all the other commitments I made. This was not cool.

So now, I sit and give in to serenity in order to maintain calm and reflect. It's good for the soul. Good for the heart. Great for our capacity. And if you are wondering, the answer is no. I did not rush off late to another commitment after my moment in sunny serenity.

The Rewiring Process

Rewiring our zones of genius and moments of brilliance is like redrawing a map: it's intricate and demanding, often leaving you more lost than when you began. Many of us thrive under pressure, using looming deadlines and stress as fuel to produce our best work. It's how we're programmed. Yet most of us lack a contingency plan for when we run out of time or face major interruptions. This high-pressure zone is a tunnel of focus, a gold mine of ideas and output. The adrenaline from performing under tight deadlines gives us the energy to succeed. However, success often comes with a cost, producing an aftermath that's messy and sometimes irresponsible. Many of us struggle to reprogram our approach to achieving goals in a healthier way.

Surrender to your preferred ways of working by minimizing guilt and shame. Instead of trying to rework habits that may drastically reduce your output and be counterintuitive to your process, why not manage the expectations of others regarding your methods and needs? We constantly seek quick strategies to optimize, be better and do more, faster, while minimizing pain and discomfort, often being sold solutions to fix our habits. Why not invest in our own process and honor our unique ways of working?

This is what Capacity Creator is all about: gaining a deeper understanding of the factors that influence us and creating a comfortable environment to have conversations about our needs. By doing so, we empower ourselves to ask for what we require to thrive, all while maintaining our commitments in a sustainably ambitious manner. Capacity Creator encourages us to align our work habits with our values, ensuring that our approach to productivity is both effective and respectful of our well-being. It helps foster a culture where open dialogue and mutual respect lead to healthier, more sustainable success.

Stories of Impact Through Capacity Management

Understanding and respecting my own capacity has been a transformative journey, one that has not only shaped my personal and professional life but also profoundly impacted those I work with. Through the principles of capacity management and the tools I've developed, I've witnessed remarkable changes in the lives of many individuals. These stories serve as powerful testaments to the effectiveness of my approach, demonstrating how a clear understanding of one's limits and potential can lead to meaningful and sustainable success. Allow me to share three examples of people who have experienced significant improvements in their lives through our work together.

I Was a Jerk!

A man named Grayson attending my keynote approached me afterward, saying, "Thank you for your talk on Capacity and Egocake."

"My pleasure, thank you," I replied. "What resonated the most?"

"You prompted me to do something really important."

"What was that?" I asked.

"I texted my fiancée to apologize. I was a total and absolute jerk last week."

"I see. Curious to know more."

"I was raw from a couple of weeks of seriously overcapacitating."

"Well, that is some solid self-awareness!"

"I came home and unleashed on my partner. It wasn't fair to her. So, I just texted her to apologize for being an ass."

"How did she react?" I inquired.

"She was so appreciative. But I was humbled and reminded that I do so much for everyone else, it leaves little capacity for my relationship."

"Thank you for sharing your story," I said, placing my hand on my heart. "Why is it that those we love the most get to experience the worst of us because of everything we give to everyone else? Guilty of this? Let's change this, shall we?"

A Room Full of Volunteers

I recall being asked to speak for a prominent volunteer organization. Excitedly, I prepared my keynote with statistics about how amazing volunteers are and the power of community. I had fun things planned and couldn't wait to speak. The day arrived, and I packed my bags, arriving at the location with enthusiasm. As people started filing into the room, I noticed something surprising: the average age of the attendees was over seventy. Many of them were decorated war veterans with medallions. They had been serving their communities and countries for a long time and continued to volunteer.

I was stunned and thought, *Should I pack up and run? What the heck am I going to teach these phenomenal men and women?* But I decided to stick to the script.

As I gave my keynote, I noticed some head nodding. No, they were not falling asleep; they were nodding in agreement. This gave me so much energy and encouragement, seeing that I was reaching people of this caliber.

After the talk, I packed up my bags, spoke to a few people, and headed out the door. As I was leaving for my car, I heard an older man's powerful, stern voice call out, "Young lady!"

I turned around, hesitantly replying, "Yes, sir?" in a tone that was like speaking to a commander.

He said, "You made me think tonight."

"Oh? How so?" I asked.

"I'm on five committees, have six grandchildren, and drive an hour each way to get to those," he said.

"Wow," I responded.

He continued, "You made me realize something tonight."

"Ok, what's that?" I asked.

"That's not easy for people to do," he said. "You made me realize that I've been asked to be on another committee, and I am giving myself permission to say, 'No, I don't have the capacity for another committee.'"

"That is fantastic," I said.

"Thank you," he said, and walked away.

This story showcases that it doesn't matter what age you are; taking a look at your capacity and spending time to understand where you might feel stretched or overwhelmed don't have to be another chore. It just takes a little reflection. I've made it easy for people to evaluate what they're doing and where they might feel stretched, giving them the language and permission to say no, and helping them optimize their capacity.

I have felt this in my bones. I've been through burnout and mental health crises. I created these tools not only to help myself but to help others. I'm honored to be doing this work.

Not Just Another Three - Step Process: A Lifelong Practice of Capacity Management

"Buckle up."

"Suck it up."

"Get it done."

Maybe you've said these things to your team or, have heard it from the top.

Last year, I stood before forty executives in a workshop for an international company, all accustomed to the relentless pace of business. The director spoke about the health of the company—profits, partnerships, forecasts—but not once mentioned the health of his team. Half the room was on the verge of burnout. The VP of HR confided in me, worried they'd lose key people any day. As they looked at me for answers, I could see the exhaustion in their eyes. This wasn't a situation for a quick fix or a simple three-step process. Managing capacity is a lifelong practice, not a formula.

I introduced them to the Burnout Prevention Method, a holistic approach to balancing professional and personal life. We explored the Egocake framework, guiding them through overwhelming options, distractions, and commitments. Together, we identified what truly mattered beyond the numbers and deadlines. They listed their top roles, associated goals, and meaningful measures of success. We discussed the importance of letting go of commitments that no longer aligned with their values.

As the workshop progressed, tension gave way to laughter, and camaraderie grew. The executives began sharing stories—not just about work, but about their lives, passions, and dreams. They realized that managing capacity wasn't about squeezing more into their schedules but about making conscious choices that aligned with their values and energy.

By the end of the day, they saw capacity management as more than surviving the business grind, but thriving in all aspects of life, embracing a sustainable ambition that honored their well-being and that of their team. They left with a renewed perspective—not another three-step process to follow, but a lifelong practice to master.

As we conclude this journey, remember that this is just the beginning. Capacity management isn't a destination but a continuous adventure. Embrace the lessons, tools, and insights you've gained. Let them guide you as you navigate the complexities of modern life, balancing ambition with well-being and purpose with passion. This is your call to action: to live fully, thrive, and inspire others to do the same. Thrive beyond functioning burnout: find balance in your energy, embrace your purpose, and nurture your community.

Installing a Capacity Management Mindset within Our Children

In a recent interview, I was asked about some of the creative ways I've seen people apply the capacity management strategies I've developed. The question gave me pause, but as I reflected, I recalled numerous personal emails, reposted content, messages of gratitude, and even photos sent to me long after I had delivered a keynote speech. These examples often bring tears to my eyes and make my heart swell with pride.

One particularly moving email came from a woman who attended one of my keynotes. She wrote:

"Dear Melanie, I attended your keynote three weeks ago, came home, and introduced the notion of capacity to my family. At first, they kind of looked at me with their heads tilted, but I am so pleased to report back that my child has started using the word *capacity* in his vocabulary to express how tired he is from sports. This led to a level-headed conversation that helped me understand and give my child the language to express how he was feeling. I can't thank you enough. Capacity is now part of our family discussions."

When I received this email, I think I reread it ten times. It was a powerful testament to the impact of changing our language. Often, when we say, "I just don't have the time," we lack the words to fully convey our feelings, which diminishes the significance of what we're trying to express. This woman's child, a ten-year-old, had been trying to communicate his exhaustion and need for support. Understanding and using the word *capacity* gave him a way to articulate his physical, mental, and emotional depletion. This story highlights the profound impact of integrating capacity management into everyday life. By adopting and tweaking our language, we can create new dimensions of expression and understanding within our families and communities.

Capacity: A Holistic Approach

Imagine you start your day differently. Instead of just looking at a task list, you use the 3x3 method to evaluate the broader context of your capacity. You begin by assessing your overall energy levels, both physical and mental. You realize you are feeling a bit worn out from a busy week.

With this awareness, you decide to structure your day to balance high-energy tasks with restorative activities. You schedule the urgent report for the morning when your energy is highest. After the report, you take a fifteen-minute break, using the load management tool. For the meeting, you ensure it's scheduled for a time when you feel alert but not rushed, allowing for more effective engagement.

Throughout the day, you use the CHIEFF of Your Capacity tool to monitor your capacity in various areas: Career, Health, Intellectual, Emotional, Financial, Fun, with Spirituality and Family intertwined. You notice your emotional capacity is low, so you schedule a quick chat with a colleague to boost your mood. By the end of the day, you have not only completed your tasks but also managed your energy levels, preventing burnout. Using these tools, you have balanced your workload in a way that respects your overall capacity.

Through these stories, we see how prioritization alone, while efficient in handling tasks, can lead to burnout if not managed within the broader context of an individual's capacity. By integrating capacity management tools, you not only complete tasks but also maintain a healthy, balanced approach to your overall workload. This holistic method ensures sustainable productivity, well-being, and long-term success.

Latest Diary Entry

The warm glow of the setting sun reflects off the pool, creating soft, shimmering patterns on the water. A gentle breeze stirs the air, carrying the scent of fresh herbs and the sizzle of dinner off the grill. My family's laughter floats around me, a joyful soundtrack that makes the rest of the world fade into the background.

As I settle into the cushioned chair by the pool, the familiar buzz of my cellphone interrupts the tranquility. I glance at the screen—an email from work, another request, another decision to be made. For a brief moment, the old instinct tugs at my chest, the urge to answer, to be available, to say yes. But then, I remember the promise I made, not just to my family but to myself.

With a calm, deliberate motion, I press the button to lock my screen and dismiss the message. The world can wait. Tonight is about more than just dinner: it's about presence, about honoring the space I've fought to create for myself and those I love. It's about recognizing that true balance isn't a perfect equation, but a series of choices that align with what truly matters.

As I put the phone down, I feel a sense of peace wash over me. I look at the faces around me—my family, my anchors, my joy—and I realize that this is what balance looks like. Not a constant juggling act, but a harmonious flow where work and life complement each other, where I can be fully present in both, without sacrificing either.

The journey to get here hasn't been easy, but it has been worth every step. And as I take a deep breath, inhaling the rich tapestry of this evening, I know that the journey is far from over. There are more lessons to learn, more discoveries to be made, more balance to fine-tune.

For now, though, I'm exactly where I need to be—in this moment, by the pool, with the people who matter the most. And as the sun dips below the horizon, painting the sky with shades of twilight, I feel a sense of excitement for what lies ahead.

This may be the last page of this chapter, but the story continues. There's always more to explore, more to share, and I have a feeling that the next chapter might just be the most exciting yet. Until then, I'll be right here honoring my capacity, finding my balance, and embracing the beautiful complexity of it all.

With gratitude, and determination to write another book,
Melanie

This page is intentionally left blank for you to capture some notes, thoughts, and reflections on what we've covered in Part 3: Honor Your Capacity.

Bibliography

- American Psychological Association. "Multitasking: Switching Costs." *American Psychological Association*, 20 Mar. 2006, https://www.apa.org/topics/research/multitasking

- Andrew, Mari [bymariandrew]. *Instagram*, https://www.instagram.com/bymariandrew/.

- Anthony, Scott D. "The Planning Fallacy and the Innovator's Dilemma." *Harvard Business Review*, 1 Aug. 2012, https://hbr.org/2012/08/the-planning-fallacy-and-the-i.

- Attridge, Mark. "Employee Assistance Programs: Evidence and Current Trends." *Handbook of Occupational Health and Wellness*, edited by Robert J. Gatchel and Izabella Z. Schultz, Springer, 2012, pp. 441–67.

- Baumeister, Roy F., and John Tierney. *Willpower: Rediscovering the Greatest Human Strength*. Penguin, 2011.

- Benefits Canada. "79% of Canadians Would Use Mental-health Services More If Cost Wasn't a Factor: Survey." *Benefits Canada*, 22 May 2024, https://www.benefitscanada.com/benefits/health-wellness/79-of-canadians-would-use-mental-health-services-more-if-cost-wasnt-a-factor-survey/.

- Bode, Stefan, et al. "Tracking the Unconscious Generation of Free Decisions Using Ultra-High Field fMRI." *PLOS ONE*, vol. 6, no. 6, June 27, 2011, e21612, https://doi.org/10.1371/journal.pone.0021612.

- Brown, Brené. *Daring Greatly: How the Courage to Be Vulnerable Transforms the Way We Live, Love, Parent, and Lead*. Gotham, 2015.

- Canadian Institute for Health Information. "Canadians Report Increasing Need for Mental Health Care Alongside Barriers to Access." *Canadian Institute for Health Information*, Mar. 21,

2024, https://www.cihi.ca/en/canadians-report-increasing-need-for-mental-health-care-alo ngside-barriers-to-access.

- Clear, James. *Atomic Habits: An Easy & Proven Way to Build Good Habits & Break Bad Ones.* Avery, 2018.

- Common Sense. *Technology Addiction: Concern, Controversy, and Finding Balance.* Common Sense, 3 May 2016, https://www.commonsensemedia.org/research/technology-addiction-concern-c ontroversy-and-finding-balance.

- Davenport, Thomas H, and John C. Beck. *The Attention Economy: Understanding the New Currency of Business.* Harvard Business Review Press, 2001.

- De Hert, Stefan. "Burnout in Healthcare Workers: Prevalence, Impact and Preventative Strate- gies." *Local and Regional Anesthesia*, vol. 13, 2020, pp. 171–83, https://doi.org/10.2147/LRA.S 240564.

- Deloitte. *2018 Global Mobile Consumer Survey: A New Era in Mobile Continues.* US Ed. Deloitte, 2018, https://www2.deloitte.com/content/dam/Deloitte/us/Documents/technology-media-t elecommunications/us-tmt-global-mobile-consumer-survey-exec-summary-2018.pdf.

- Deloitte. *Workplace Burnout Survey.* Deloitte, 2019, https://www2.deloitte.com/us/en/pages/a bout-deloitte/articles/burnout-survey.html.

- Dscout. *Mobile Touches: Dscout's Inaugural Study on Humans and Their Tech.* Dscout, 15 June 2016, https://pages.dscout.com/hubfs/downloads/dscout_mobile_touches_study_2016.pdf?_ ga=2.180416224.67221035.1650551540-199217915.1650551540.

- GWI. *Social: GWI's Flagship Report on the Latest Trends in Social Media.* GWI, 2021, https://www .gwi.com/hubfs/Downloads/Social%20Media%20Report%20-%20GWI.pdf.

- GWI. *Social Media Trends in 2019.* GWI, 2019, https://www.gwi.com/reports/social-2019.

- Hanisch, Sabine E., et al. "The Effectiveness of Interventions Targeting the Stigma of Mental Illness at the Workplace: A Systematic Review." *BMC Psychiatry*, vol. 16, 2016, 1.

- Hanley-Dafoe, Robyne. *Calm Within the Storm: A Pathway to Everyday Resiliency.* Page Two Books, 2021.

- Hanley-Dafoe, Robyne, *Stressing Wisely: How to Build a Resilient Life by Managing Stress*. Page Two Books, 2023.

- Hanley-Dafoe, Robyne. "My Interview with Dr Robyne Hanley-Dafoe." Interview by Melanie Sodka. *Hustle Hypocrisy*, Sept. 14, 2024, *YouTube*, https://www.youtube.com/watch?v=XbHOkf KQA6k.

- Hardy, Benjamin. *Be Your Future Self Now: The Science of Intentional Transformation*. Hay House Business, 2022.

- He, Amy. "Average US Time Spent with Mobile in 2019 Has Increased." *EMARKETER*, 4 June 2019, https://www.emarketer.com/content/average-us-time-spent-with-mobile-in-2019-has -increased.

- Hendricks, Gay. *The Big Leap: Conquer Your Hidden Fear and Take Life to the Next Level*. HarperOne, 2009.

- Herman, Todd. *The Alter Ego Effect: The Power of Secret Identities to Transform Your Life*. Harper Business, 2019.

- Holiday, Ryan. *Ego Is the Enemy*. Portfolio, 2016.

- Housel, Morgan. *The Psychology of Money: Timeless Lessons on Wealth, Greed, and Happiness*. Harriman House, 2020.

- "How to Stress Wisely and Heal from Burnout and Compassion Fatigue." *Speakers Spotlight*, Sept 9, 2021, https://www.speakers.ca/2021/09/how-to-stress-wisely-and-heal-from-burnou t-and-compassion-fatigue/.

- Hutto, Cara. "Why We Should All Resolve to Ditch Hustle Culture." *InHerSight*, https://www.in hersight.com/blog/work-life-balance/hustle-culture.

- Hylant. "Improving Utilization of Employee Assistance Programs." *Hylant*, 15 Feb. 2024, https: //hylant.com/insights/blog/improving-utilization-of-employee-assistance-programs

- Janssen, Christian P. "Integrating Knowledge of Multitasking and Interruptions across Different Perspectives and Research Methods." *International Journal of Human-Computer Studies*, vol. 79, July 2015, pp. 1–5, https://doi.org/10.1016/j.ijhcs.2015.03.002.

- Jiménez, Jacinta M. *The Burnout Fix: Overcome Overwhelm, Beat Busy, and Sustain Success in the New World of Work.* McGraw Hill, 2021.

- Johnson, Spencer. *Peaks and Valleys: Making Good and Bad Times Work for You—at Work and in Life.* Atria Books, 2009.

- Kemp, Simon. "The Time We Spend on Social Media." *DataReportal*, 31 Jan. 2024, https://datareportal.com/reports/digital-2024-deep-dive-the-time-we-spend-on-social-media.

- Khan, Asaduzzaman, et al. "Excessive Smartphone Use is Associated with Depression, Anxiety, Stress, and Sleep Quality of Australian Adults." *Journal of Medical Systems*, vol. 47, no. 1, 2023, 109, https://doi.org/10.1007/s10916-023-02005-3.

- LePera, Nicole. *How to Do the Work: Recognize Your Patterns, Heal from Your Past, and Create Your Self.* Harper, 2021.

- Marie, Simone. "'Toxic Positivity' Is Real—and It's a Big Problem During the Pandemic." *Healthline*, 4 July 2023, https://www.healthline.com/health/mental-health/toxic-positivity-during-the-pandemic.

- Mark, Gloria, et al. "The Cost of Interrupted Work: More Speed and Stress." *CHI '08: Proceedings of the SIGCHI Conference on Human Factors in Computing Systems*, 6 Apr. 2008, pp. 107–10, https://doi.org/10.1145/1357054.1357072.

- Mark, Gloria, et al. "Email Duration, Batching and Self-interruption: Patterns of Email Use on Productivity and Stress." *CHI '16: Proceedings of the 2016 CHI Conference on Human Factors in Computing Systems*, 7 May 2016, pp. 1717–28, https://doi.org/10.1145/2858036.2858262.

- Mark, Gloria, et al. "No Task Left Behind?: Examining the Nature of Fragmented Work." *CHI '05: Proceedings of the SIGCHI Conference on Human Factors in Computing Systems*, 2 Apr. 2005, pp. 321–30, https://dl.acm.org/doi/10.1145/1054972.1055017.

- Maslach, Christina, and Michael P. Leiter. "How to Measure Burnout Accurately and Ethically." *Harvard Business Review*, 19 Mar. 2021, https://hbr.org/2021/03/how-to-measure-burnout-accurately-and-ethically.

- Maslach, Christina, and Susan E. Jackson. "The Measurement of Experienced Burnout." *Journal of Organizational Behavior*, vol. 2, issue 2, 1981, pp. 99–113, https://doi.org/10.1002/job.4030020205.

- Maté, Gabor. *When the Body Says No: The Cost of Hidden Stress.* Knopf, 2003.

- Mental Health America. "How Can We Promote Our EAP to Increase Its Usage?" *Mental Health America*, https://www.mhanational.org/how-can-we-promote-our-eap-increase-its-usage.

- Microsoft Canada. *Attention Spans.* 2015, https://dl.motamem.org/microsoft-attention-spans-research-report.pdf.

- Nagoski, Emily, and Amelia Nagoski. *Burnout: The Secret to Unlocking the Stress Cycle.* Ballantine, 2019.

- Nielsen. *The Nielsen Total Audience Report: April 2020.* Nielsen, Apr. 2020, https://www.nielsen.com/insights/2020/the-nielsen-total-audience-report-april-2020/.

- Orgad, Shanni. "Working 9-to-5 Then 5-to-9: 'Hustle Culture' for Women during a Global Pandemic." *Media@LSE*, February 11, 2021, https://blogs.lse.ac.uk/medialse/2021/02/11/working-9-to-5-then-5-to-9-hustle-culture-for-women-during-a-global-pandemic/.

- Otting, Laura Gassner. "HH Episode 3 – Laura Gassner-Otting." Interview by Melanie Sodka. *Hustle Hypocrisy*, Spotify, https://open.spotify.com/episode/3UGwPxeHz2NwygTLdcvGOQ?si=ad98c365cd6e4baa

- Otting, Laura Gassner. *Limitless: How to Ignore Everybody, Carve your Own Path, and Live Your Best Life.* Ideapress, 2019.

- Otting, Laura Gassner. *Wonderhell: Why Success Doesn't Feel Like It Should ... and What to Do about It.* Ideapress, 2023.

- Pesce, Nicole Lyn. "The Average Worker Checks Their Email Before They Even Get Out of Bed in the Morning." *MarketWatch*, 9 Feb. 2019, https://www.marketwatch.com/story/the-average-worker-checks-their-email-before-they-even-get-out-of-bed-in-the-morning-2019-02-06.

- Pielot, Martin, et al. "An In-situ Study of Mobile Phone Notifications." *MobileHCI '14: Proceedings of the 16th International Conference on Human-computer Interaction with Mobile Devices and Services*, 23 Sept. 2014, pp. 233–42, https://doi.org/10.1145/2628363.2628364.

- Radicati Group. *Email Statistics Report, 2021–2025.* Radicati Group, 2021, https://www.radicati.com/wp/wp-content/uploads/2020/12/Email-Statistics-Report-2021-2025-Executive-Summary.pdf.

- Robbins, Mel. *The 5 Second Rule: The Fastest Way to Change Your Life.* Savio Republic, 2017.

- Sana Counselling. "How Much Does Therapy Cost in Canada?" *Sana Counselling*, Feb. 17, 2023, https://depression.informedchoices.ca/types-of-treatment/counseling-or-therapy/how-much-does-therapy-or-counseling-cost/

- Sana Counselling. : "Counselling Fees and Direct Billing" *Sana Counselling, https://sanapsychological.com/fees/*

- Sawhney, Vasundhara. *It's Okay to Not Be Okay.* Harvard Business Review, 2020.

- Schwartz, Barry. "The Paradox of Choice." *TEDGlobal*, July 2005, https://www.ted.com/talks/barry_schwartz_the_paradox_of_choice.

- Schwartz, Barry. *The Paradox of Choice: Why More Is Less.* Ecco, 2004.

- Sharma, Robin S. *The Monk Who Sold His Ferrari: A Spiritual Fable about Fulfilling Your Dreams and Reaching Your Destiny.* HarperCollins Canada, 1997.

- *16Personalities.* NERIS Analytics Limited, 2024, https://www.16personalities.com/.

- Sodka, Melanie. "Burnout: How Addiction to Distraction Is Eroding Our Capacity." *TEDxWindsor*, June 2019, https://www.ted.com/talks/melanie_sodka_burnout_how_addiction_to_distraction_is_eroding_our_capacity?subtitle=en.

- Sodka, Melanie. "Hustle They Say." *YouTube*, 17 July 2022. https://www.youtube.com/watch?v=Mdyw6HD2hk8

- Soon, Chun Siong, et al. "Unconscious Determinants of Free Decisions in the Human Brain." *Nature Neuroscience*, vol. 11, issue 5, May 2008, pp. 543–45.

- Therapy Alberta. "Resources & Insurance for Counselling & Therapy." *Therapy Alberta*, https://www.therapyalberta.com/insurance-counselling-alberta.

- Tonkin, Lois. "Growing around Grief—Another Way of Looking at Grief and Recovery." *Bereavement Care*, vol. 15, issue 1, 1996, p. 10.

- Vaynerchuk, Gary. GaryVaynerchuk.com "Hustle: The Cure for those Who Complain." July 3, 2017. https://garyvaynerchuk.com/hustle-cure-complain/

- Vohs, Kathleen D., et al. "Making Choices Impairs Subsequent Self-control: A Limited-resource Account of Decision Making, Self-regulation, and Active Initiative." *Journal of Personality and Social Psychology*, vol. 94, issue 5, May 2008, pp. 883–98, https://doi.org/10.1037/0022-3514.94.5.883.

- World Health Organization. "Mental Health in the Workplace—Information Sheet." *Communications Workers Union, Equality, Education, and Development*, 2017, https://education.cwu.org/wp-content/uploads/2017/10/Mental-health-in-the-workplace-Information-Sheet-WHO.pdf. Originally published by WHO, 2017.

- Wu, Tim. *The Attention Merchants: The Epic Scramble to Get Inside Our Heads*. Vintage, 2017.

Acknowledgments

There are so many people who have played a significant role in making this book a reality, and I want to express my deepest gratitude to each of them.

To my husband, Chris—your unwavering support, belief in me, and constant encouragement have lifted me up at every step of this journey. Thank you for always being my rock and for believing in this project.

To my amazing children—you are not only my greatest cheerleaders but also my accountability partners. Your love, energy, and enthusiasm keep me motivated and grounded every single day.

To my parents—thank you for raising me to be the woman I am today. Your strength, guidance, and love have shaped who I am, and I am forever grateful.

To my immediate family and in-laws—thank you for your ongoing support and thoughtfulness, which made the process so much easier and enjoyable! Special thanks for the delicious treats when I was working out of your home office to borrow your internet.

To my best friends, who are like the sisters I never had and the family we chose to be—thank you for always asking, listening, and encouraging me. Your constant love and support were felt throughout this journey.

A heartfelt thank you to Clifton Corbin, whose early support, consulting, and belief in this project, along with his invaluable guardrails, ensured it was completed on time. To Wayne Jones, I am deeply grateful for your editing expertise, patience, and the humor you infused throughout the past three years. Blake Fly, thank you for helping me sift through years of notes, journal entries, and ideas, and for seeing the future of this project even before I could. To Chris Farias, your creative contribution to the cover of the book and my many projects over the years, has been so much fun! To my advance readers, your thoughtful feedback in such a short amount of time was an enormous task, and I truly appreciate your commitment to this journey. To my corporate lawyer Andrian Lozinksi who always has my back.

To my academic community and friends, we are blessed to help shape the future. To my entrepreneurial community in Niagara and the GTHA– it's an absolute privilege to be part of your start-up journeys and scaling endeavours.

To the Dovetail community, especially Alexis Dean—your support and motivation were instrumental in bringing this project to life. Your generous and inspiring community showed me what's possible when I fully commit to following my dreams.

To my therapist. Thank you for guiding me through this journey of healing and self-discovery. Your support has been invaluable in helping me reclaim my capacity and find balance.

About the Author

Melanie Sodka is an accomplished capacity management expert, author, and speaker with a deep passion for helping individuals and teams navigate the complexities of modern work life.

Drawing from over two decades of experience in corporate environments and as a professor of entrepreneurship, Melanie has dedicated her career to developing innovative frameworks that empower people to honor their capacity, prevent burnout, and achieve sustainable success.

As the founder of Capacity Creator Corporation, Melanie has created transformative tools such as the Egocake framework, Capacity Elasticity, Healthy Hustle Awards, the Foresee App and the Burnout Prevention Method program, all designed to guide individuals through the challenges of overwhelming workloads and constant distractions. Her work centers on the belief that true productivity and fulfillment stem from understanding and managing one's capacity, rather than simply striving for more.

Melanie's insights have been shaped by her own journey through burnout, which inspired her to reimagine how we approach work, commitments, and well-being. Her personal experience with grief and resilience has further enriched her perspective, making her guidance deeply empathetic and relatable.

In addition to her consulting and coaching practice, Melanie is the host of the *Hustle Hypocrisy* podcast, where she explores the nuances of hustle culture and its impact on our lives. She has also founded the Good Grief Gala, an innovative fundraiser event designed to address and explore the multifaceted nature of grief.

Melanie's work has resonated with audiences across various industries, from to corporate leaders to start-ups, helping foster environments where people can thrive without sacrificing their well-being. Through her writing, speaking engagements, and workshops, Melanie continues to inspire others to break free from the relentless pace of modern life and embrace a more balanced, meaningful approach to their personal and professional lives.

Diary of a Functioning Burnout: How to Honor Your Capacity and Balance Your Life is her first book. It offers readers a candid and practical guide to reclaiming their energy, purpose, and connection.

Connect with Melanie on:

www.melaniesodka.com

https://www.linkedin.com/in/melanie-sodka

https://www.instagram.com/melaniesodka/

www.ingramcontent.com/pod-product-compliance
Lightning Source LLC
Chambersburg PA
CBHW051258020426
42333CB00026B/3253